LESSONS

In

DELIVERANCE

love you in so many ways!
Mom

by Susan J Perry

"Deliverance comes to only those with a want to!"

Copyright Page

© 2021 Susan J Perry

First Printing

All rights reserved. Reproduction in whole or part without written permission from the publisher or author is strictly prohibited. Printed in the United States of America.

All Scripture is taken from several versions of the Holy Bible, public domain

This book is inspired by the Holy Spirit
Who teaches us all things!

Susan J Perry
Edgewater, Florida

Simply This Publishing
Kindle Direct Publishing

Cover Picture © Sergey Nivens/Adobe Stock

*"GOD said it,
I didn't,
GOD told me to tell you!"*

~ Susan J. Perry ~

Matthew 14:22-29

Jesus Walks on the Sea

²² Immediately Jesus made His disciples get into the boat and go before Him to the other side, while He sent the multitudes away.

²³ And when He had sent the multitudes away, He went up on the mountain by Himself to pray. Now when evening came, He was alone there.

²⁴ But the boat was now in the middle of the sea, tossed by the waves, for the wind was contrary.

²⁵ Now in the fourth watch of the night Jesus went to them, walking on the sea.

²⁶ And when the disciples saw Him walking on the sea, they were troubled, saying, "It is a ghost!" And they cried out for fear.

²⁷ But immediately Jesus spoke to them, saying, "Be of good cheer! It is I; do not be afraid."

²⁸ And Peter answered Him and said, "Lord, if it is You, command me to come to You on the water."

²⁹ So He said, "Come." And when Peter had come down out of the boat, he walked on the water to go to Jesus.

DEDICATION

My whole world, my whole life is dedicated to you Father God, Jesus Christ the Son and the Holy Spirit and power of the Godhead and so is this book. It is yours. It was your idea and I pray I can do this topic justice because this is a difficult one out there in the church world and the world in general. There will be a lot of battles fought and won by you. So I stand by your side and do what you tell me and write what you say write. I know you give a lot of freedom in our writings but I also am given teaching and direction by the Holy Spirit and I pray to stay obedient in your eyes.

It's all about You Lord; our writings should reflect you in every way and at every angle. This book is yours and I wait upon you for further instruction and I know you will set me straight on that narrow path where few dare to go. Thank You Lord for all of your precious gifts given freely and lovingly and thank you for wisdom, please give me more wisdom on this topic. I need wisdom. Many need pure deliverance today because the days are waning and your return is imminent and we must get cleaned up as your people and as your bride. The church must know and use deliverance to help its cause. How as the church, can we help others if we need help ourselves? Jesus said that He is the way, now as we follow Him we expect deliverance topics and experiences to cause others to stop and think about their own lives. We must be a bride without spot or wrinkle. The church needs deliverance!

Help us oh Lord get set free!

"Oh God 1-2-3 deliverance is for me! We must wait, we must pray, continue on this journey, so all may see!"

INTRODUCTION

God began this book in a dream state during an afternoon nap as I dreamed about deliverance. He showed me the Light of His presence will deliver the darkness. Now this sounds very simple doesn't it? There is light in everything God does. We must now be the light as God shines through us and uses us. Today He is trying to use us in deliverance. The church needs this help. Thinking of the Ten Commandments today, in question: *"Are we keeping what God has given us?"*

If we study the Ten Commandments, the law given to Moses by God up on Mt. Sinai, we wonder if we can keep these simplistic commandments. There are only ten of these but the Bible says if we break one we break them all. Imagine that? Can you keep all of these?

Exodus 20:2-17
The Ten Commandments:

2 I am the LORD thy God, which have brought thee out of the land of Egypt, out of the house of bondage.

3 Thou shalt have no other gods before me.

4 Thou shalt not make unto thee any graven image, or any likeness of any thing that is in heaven above, or that is in the earth beneath, or that is in the water under the earth.

5 Thou shalt not bow down thyself to them, nor serve them: for I the Lord thy God am a jealous God, visiting the iniquity of the fathers upon the children unto the third and fourth generation of them that hate me;

6 And shewing mercy unto thousands of them that love me, and keep my commandments.

7 Thou shalt not take the name of the Lord thy God in vain; for the Lord will not hold him guiltless that taketh his name in vain.

8 Remember the Sabbath day, to keep it holy.

9 Six days shalt thou labour, and do all thy work:

10 But the seventh day is the sabbath of the Lord thy God: in it thou shalt not do any work, thou, nor thy son, nor thy daughter, thy manservant, nor thy maidservant, nor thy cattle, nor thy stranger that is within thy gates:

11 For in six days the Lord made heaven and earth, the sea, and all that in them is, and rested the seventh day: wherefore the Lord blessed the sabbath day, and hallowed it.

12 Honour thy father and thy mother: that thy days may be long upon the land which the Lord thy God giveth thee.

13 Thou shalt not kill.

14 Thou shalt not commit adultery.

15 Thou shalt not steal.

16 Thou shalt not bear false witness against thy neighbour.

17 Thou shalt not covet thy neighbour's house, thou shalt not covet thy neighbour's wife, nor his manservant, nor his maidservant, nor his ox, nor his ass, nor any thing that is thy neighbour's.

  Have you ever broken one of these laws? Of course you have and we depend on the grace of God to sustain us because Jesus died on the cross to save us from the law but we still must obey these very simple laws. Have we kept the Sabbath holy and never worked or played on it? Have you ever taken the name of the Lord in vain? Come on now be honest, God knows? Not one of us is perfect. Have you ever spoken against another with your words? This is considered murder at times? Where have you sinned against God? These are not forgotten laws, they are still pertinent today and we must obey them all. That's why Jesus came to die for us to heal and deliver us and set us free.

R-E-P-E-N-T!

2 Chronicles 7:14
If my people, which are called by my name, shall humble themselves, and pray, and seek my face, and turn from their wicked ways; then will I hear from heaven, and will forgive their sin, and will heal their land.

IF MY PEOPLE....

It all depends on us. We must want to be delivered! We must know we are hurting and get some help! I hope we can help you in this book and open your eyes and heart to deliverance. God says many are fearful of deliverance! Yes they want to be set free but are afraid of the admittance of their weakness. The Bible says:

2 Corinthians 13:9
For we are glad, when we are weak, and ye are strong: and this also we wish, even your perfection.

Open up and speak to someone you trust and seek God's help in guiding you. We all need deliverance from time to time from the things of the world because we are in the world but we are not of the world. (John 8:23)

Become a proponent of healing and deliverance. Be the one who lays hands on the sick and they will be healed. But first you must get yourself cleaned up. Proponent is God's word, what does it mean?

pro·po·nent

/prəˈpōnənt/

Noun

- 1. a person who advocates a theory, proposal, or project:

Pray in tongues until you get all the answers. Fast and pray until you hear from God. Be desperate until you become that proponent of victory! I hope we can help you in these writings of lessons on deliverance given by the Holy Spirit. It is not an easy topic but must be told and must be bold to heal and deliver what is foreign in your body, mind, will and emotions.

CHAPTER CONTENTS

Dedication
Page 6

Introduction
Page 8

Special Thanks...
Page 17

**The Year 2021
The Year of Great Deliverance**
Page 20

Lesson #1: The Light
Page 26

Lesson #2: The Presence
Page 33

Lesson # 3: Your Will
Page 41

Lesson # 4: Your Heart
Page 48

Lesson # 5: Thanksgiving
Page 55

Lesson # 6: Communion
Page 62

Lesson # 7: Praise & Worship
Page 65

Lesson # 8: Inner Healing & Deliverance
Page 72

Lesson # 9: Fear Must Go! Faith Must Come!
Page 81

Lesson # 10: The All Consuming Fire
Page 90

Lesson # 11: Always Pray for Your Friends
Page 97

Lesson # 12: Deliverance is Like a Shipwreck
Page 105

Lesson # 13: The Heart of the Father is Love
Page 109

Lesson # 14: Nothing But The Blood of Jesus
Page 115

Lesson # 15: The Name of JESUS Will Deliver You!
Page 121

Lesson # 16: The Lesson on Counseling
Page 127

Lesson # 17: Even the Angels Will Help You
Page 136

Lesson # 18: Deliverance from Worldliness
Page 144

Lesson # 19: Demons, Devils and Deliverances
Page 155

Lesson # 20: Killing the Fruit of Cancer
Page 162

Lesson # 21: Deliverance from Bullies
Page 173

Lesson # 22: Whomsoever
Page 180

Lesson # 23: A Reprieve
Page 187

Author's Corner
Page 192

Perry's Book Shelf
Page 194

Special Thanks...

Frank & Karen Sumrall: God bless you both in all of your days, your support is unending and faithful. We love you very much! Your examples in the Body of Christ have been enduring and filled with love and joy! Thank you for all you do for all of us! I repent for those who have mistreated you and could not see the gifts in you, in Jesus mighty name!! Your names are before the Lord of Heaven continuously and He sees your hearts.

Donald & Lorraine Knapp: Thanks for both of you who prophesied this book over me until God gave me the dream and I jotted it down in this computer to begin the work of Deliverance. In Christ we have been set free but some still are tangled in the wicked web of the world and need this free service of God. Thanks to both of you for your deep faith in Jesus to speak this word! All glory to God for His works!!

Apostle Linda & Pastor Daniel Cyr: Thank you for your ministry in healing and deliverance because you taught us well from the very beginning as we met together. You imparted into our lives immensely the Fire of God and we are deeply grateful for both of your lives. We love and honor you here today, God bless you.

Apostle Nick Pena: Thank you for all your teaching and impartation, it has not fallen down to the ground and become void. We learned and received thru your ministry of Open Heavens an abundant way to live in freedom from one Lord Jesus Christ, our healer and deliverer. Your teachings were rich and the anointed life you live was passed onto us. We will be forever grateful and hope all have grown because of what God has given you. Blessings!

Pastor John R. Perry: You know my husband has been a blessing to me and so many others all his days and as we look forward to our 15th wedding anniversary we love each other. The Lord has spoken to me many times about my husband; He has titled him and not man. Although the world does not recognize him, I see him by the Spirit of the Living God and God is well pleased with the love of John especially towards others. He is a saint in God's eyes. Thank you John for all your love and indeed we have been real helpmeets together as the Bible states in:

Genesis 2:18
And the Lord God said, It is not good that the man should be alone; I will make him an help meet for him.

Our love to all!

Matthew 10:1
And when he had called unto him his twelve disciples, he gave them power against unclean spirits, to cast them out, and to heal all manner of sickness and all manner of disease.

THE YEAR OF 2021

The Year of Great Deliverance

Genesis 45:7
And God sent me before you to preserve a posterity for you in the earth, and to save your lives by a great deliverance.

This year of 2020 as it passes claims to be the toughest year yet and as we go into 2021, we shall see evil exposed and deliverance by the Great God Almighty who will shine His light into the darkness and who loves us so much! He has spoken by the Prophets that in 2020, the word was spoken by their mouths but many did not listen but believed the lies of the enemy. The church is divided and many in fear instead of faith and unity.

We as the Body of Christ must unify under one God and one purpose to win souls to the Kingdom of God while staying Kingdom minded and standing on holy ground. Now twice God has given me Psalm 21 for this coming year of 2021. It is still the mouth that speaks from 2020 hearing the words of God's Prophets going into 2021, but the people, the church must get delivered from the lies of the enemy that they have believed. For some have actually believed the deceptions spewed from enemies of our King. Jesus is coming for a Bride without spot or wrinkle and how can that be when the church is so divided today? The election of 2020 that brought so much derision and division landmarks the church as divided because the reports are that the church voted 46% for the killers of babies party or pro-choice party let's say this to be kind here and 54% voted for the pro-life party. Now that is an obvious divide and whose side do you think God is on? He is the Creator of ALL life! Do you think He wants to dispose of it that easily? This is sin. We just did the Ten Commandments and one of them says DO NOT MURDER. His heart is obviously on the side of life. Where is the churches heart? Are you not the Bride of Christ? The Church needs deliverance; a great deliverance! It will start in the Church.

Only God's deliverance will do it and it won't be pretty as we see the goats and the sheep; the wheat and the tares taking opposing positions, there must be change! Only God can bring this change as we await His hand upon the Bride who loves and fears Him. He will have His way! God will have a united body; a United States and one that will stand for Him and Him only: "One Nation Under God!"

Let us look at Psalm 21 and see what God says in scripture for this next year:

Psalm 21

To the Chief Musician. A Psalm of David.

1 The king shall have joy in Your strength, O LORD; And in Your salvation how greatly shall he rejoice!

*2 You have given him his heart's desire,
And have not withheld the request of his lips. Selah*

*3 For You meet him with the blessings of goodness;
You set a crown of pure gold upon his head.*

*4 He asked life from You, and You gave it to him—
Length of days forever and ever.*

*5 His glory is great in Your salvation;
Honor and majesty You have placed upon him.*

*6 For You have made him most blessed forever;
You have made him exceedingly glad with Your presence.*

7 For the king trusts in the L<small>ORD</small>,
And through the mercy of the Most High he shall not be moved.

*8 Your hand will find all Your enemies;
Your right hand will find those who hate You.*

*9 You shall make them as a fiery oven in the time of Your anger;
The* L<small>ORD</small> *shall swallow them up in His wrath,
And the fire shall devour them.*

*10 Their offspring You shall destroy from the earth,
And their descendants from among the sons of men.*

*11 For they intended evil against You;
They devised a plot which they are not able to perform.*

*12 Therefore You will make them turn their back;
You will make ready Your arrows on Your string
toward their faces.*

*13 Be exalted, O Lord, in Your own strength!
We will sing and praise Your power.*

Amen.

   I believe this Psalm specifically is talking about these times we are in right now at the end of 2020 where so many are confused and shooting arrows to kill the Prophets who prophesied the Word of the Lord yet there are so many in doubt and fear. We just had an officially fraudulent election for the President in the United States of America on November 3rd, 2020 and as we are headed towards another Trump Presidency in the land, we went to bed confident and woke up the next morning with a fraud in our midst trying to take over the King's Palace before its time. Opposition came from every worldly area declaring this other candidate had won, I won't even mention his name because he is not worthy as he held onto satan's plan to overtake our country and go down in defeat. A coup d'état was in operation in America. Can you ever imagine this? Now is the time for victory instead by praying and fasting, by seeking the Lord while He may still be found. The enemy is roaming around as a roaring lion seeking whom he may devour and he is very mistaken if he thinks it is his time to do so. God's plan will always supersede the plan of the enemy and we win as God's people for the result will come as a surprise to many!

Isaiah 55:6
Seek the LORD while He may be found, Call upon Him while He is near.

Pray and seek God; join forces with His Heavenly Hosts who will bring the victory once and for all as we wait upon the Lord now and be of good courage. We are in God's hand, His righteous right hand.

December 20, 2020

As we approach the Christmas season we are reminded we are heading into 2021, a New Year; a year of deliverance in the age to come. If you remember as you were a child waiting to be an adult, the year of 21 was a coming of age so to speak. 2021 will be such a year, a delivery for young and old and an awakening for many as they come of age in the Spirit of our Living God.

We will need to stay close to the Savior this year because although it will be 21, we cannot wander off on our own but appreciate the protection of the Father who has given us angels charge over us. (Psalm 91:11) Practice Psalm 91 in its entirety and be sure to stay close grabbing ahold of the hem of His garment our dear Jesus. You will need Him greatly!

Life and death is in the power of the tongue and we must be strategic in our declarations in 21. I encourage you all to speak life.

Today is Sunday and as we worshipped and praised our Lord and I was led back to Isaiah 10, the entire chapter for study and in it is a promise for deliverance and as we stand on God's promises we can be assured that it will happen and swiftly. So I wanted to share this with you all to settle into the New Year of 2021 asking God to give you a fresh anointing of fresh oil from Heaven and here is why:

Isaiah 10:27
It shall come to pass in that day
That his burden will be taken away from your shoulder,
And his yoke from your neck,
And the yoke will be destroyed because of the anointing oil.

Amen.

LESSON # 1

DELIVERANCE

The Light

Genesis 1:3
And God said, Let there be light: and there was light.

4 And God saw the light, that it was good: and God divided the light from the darkness.

God has been moving in my life and having His way. Lately I have been praying for people for whatever reason and they begin to cough and cough and because I have studied with a deliverance minister an Apostle of the faith, I know this is the true beginning of my deliverance ministry. I have been seeking God for the healing ministry but have neglected deliverance because it is not a pretty ministry. No one likes it but the two gifts in ministry go hand and hand. You hear this every where, healing and deliverance is the children's bread.

So as I lay down to take a nap today because I am tired my Father in Heaven starts talking to me. I have been very excited about this new gift I truly have been given and very thankful as well. Even my husband is excited because we know this is where the rubber meets the road; this is where I must roll up the sleeves of my garment and get dirty because deliverance ain't pretty as I said before but I know that many people need it. The church needs it.

John 8:12
Then spake Jesus again unto them, saying, I am the light of the world: he that followeth me shall not walk in darkness, but shall have the light of life.

  Do you see by this verse Jesus is the greatest of deliverers, He is the Light. He says so in this verse. As the Holy Spirit spoke to me about these verses of light, He assured me that Light will deliver the darkness; darkness will flee when light comes into the room. It cannot stay! Have you ever turned on a light switch in a room and when the light came on part of the room was still dark, or even a tiny, little part of it? No, darkness immediately goes, all of it! Did you know in heaven there is no shadow or darkness? It cannot even exist. The only reason God created day and night; light and darkness is because he knew the human body needed rest. In fact that's when God chooses to speak to me, is when I am trying to rest. He puts ideas spirit to spirit.

  This topic is very important. Many have written about it and many have taught it but the deliverance ministry is a constant spiritual battle and you must put on the full armor of God daily and be ready with the Word of God to use as our weapons towards the enemy.

  Jesus is the Light. Light is a weapon against darkness. Where does sin and degradation take place but in the darkness of the night? Seldom do you hear of blatant sin taking place in the light of day although in today's world the darkness exists within a person and they display darkness which opposes the light. All of God's children should be a light to society in the church and out. We should be a walking epistle so says Paul and I believe him.

2 Corinthians 3:2-3
Ye are our epistle written in our hearts, known and read of all men:

3 Forasmuch as ye are manifestly declared to be the epistle of Christ ministered by us, written not with ink, but with the Spirit of the living God; not in tables of stone, but in fleshy tables of the heart.

Here are two examples in the Book of John, we cannot abide in darkness or with darkness therefore deliverance will come to those around us.

John 12:36
While ye have light, believe in the light, that ye may be the children of light. These things spake Jesus, and departed, and did hide himself from them.

John 12:46
I am come a light into the world, that whosoever believeth on me should not abide in darkness.

I am only touching the Book of John here but almost every book in the Bible has mention of light in their contexts. But I like John for its simplistic nature and understanding, God is so good. He gave me this comparison as I started to sleep. Day and night, night and day two polar opposites and in deliverance the darkness must flee. God is always portrayed as embodied by great white shards of light and that's how I have seen Him and the evil one satan, the prince of the air is always pictured as black and as skulking darkness casting a demonic presence to any area, person, place or thing it inhabits, oppresses or possesses. Total polar opposites and we as followers of Jesus, the Light we should discern the difference right away because we have no business with any darkness but to cast it out immediately.

We should be people of the Light and no darkness should be in us as we read the word, pray and commune with God in a constant state of fellowship and love. God is up to something here by giving me this message. I know He has a plan and a purpose for our deliverance ministry.

Today by example I was just talking to my husband by phone and pulling into a store's parking lot so I could go in and shop. When I hung up the phone I got out of my van and locked it up walking towards the store with my purse over my shoulder. A man came out of a nearby store looked at me and startled by giving a terrible large demonic belch. His eyes got big with surprise and said,

"Oh no that wasn't me!" His words were guttural sounding! And I replied as I stared at him, "No, it wasn't me either!"

I recognized the sounds and I know this is going to happen more often. People manifest in the Light. I believe God ordained me with a mantle of deliverance the other day as I prayed over the phone with someone. There was a strong swirling presence of God all around me and it became heavier and heavier. I knew something happened then and I know now I must walk in this mantle as God gives the opportunities, I will be used.

Thank You Lord! My life is your life to be used as You will.

Get in the Light and stay there! And keep your household abiding in the Light of Jesus Christ!

2 Corinthians 6:14
Be ye not unequally yoked together with unbelievers: for what fellowship hath righteousness with unrighteousness? And what communion hath light with darkness?

This is another aspect of the light verses the darkness. Do not be unequally yoked with it because we are the children of the true Light. It's like mixing water and oil, they do not go together. The oil lies up on the top of the water because you cannot mix it together. This is talking about relationships: Man and woman, marriage and friendships; saved and unsaved. Mixing them together will not work because it is like oil and water, apples and oranges but because they are not the same it will not be a peaceable situation and bad for everyone's health involved. Light stays with light and like-mindedness and darkness agrees with more darkness until they are so inspired by the light that the switch gets turned on for them and they are converted by the light. There will be no peace until this happens.

Romans 13:12
The night is far spent, the day is at hand: let us therefore cast off the works of darkness, and let us put on the armour of light.

A Bishop friend of ours just quoted this scripture in a live video and it does pertain to this first chapter of this book because God spoke to me saying,

"The Light delivers the darkness!"

He confirmed the Word of the Lord! This is such revelation today!

John 15:7
If ye abide in me, and my words abide in you, ye shall ask what ye will, and it shall be done unto you.

LESSON # 2

DELIVERANCE

The Presence

Psalm 16:11 Thou wilt shew me the path of life: in thy presence is fulness of joy; at thy right hand there are pleasures for evermore.

The presence of God brings a shift to the atmosphere therefore causing deliverance. God's goodness and love will cause deliverance to come if you seek Him. We experienced this in our church service last night and God started speaking to me this morning before I awoke. I must know when He wants me to write. I thought I was done for awhile but I was wrong. He always wants me to write, take notes and scribe as others have done before me. God is a writer and He has proven that with me many, many times over, again and again. God is never without a word!

Last night in our services on Sunday night October 6th, 2019 we were in a worship service, which is unusual for us but we love it just the same. We could tell the Lord was headed this way and we followed. We had some very special musicians who came and visited our church here and there and mostly on Sunday nights. They carry a strong anointing in worship and the Glory of God was tangible by the time the worship was done our Bishop did not want to preach, he was happy to continue in worship. As he finally did get up to teach us more from the word, a late comer came in through the door a guest and as she did, she found a seat and started coughing and sneezing. I knew it was deliverance right away. When you are in the presence of God you cannot help but get delivered, healed and set free.

We call our church the Healing Church because when we pray corporately up at the altar together, God answers quickly. We have found the key to praying for the sick and getting great results while getting answered prayer, this is a most precious gift from God! I am always thankful about answered prayer as in James 5:16:

Confess your faults one to another, and pray one for another, that ye may be healed. The effectual fervent prayer of a righteous man availeth much.

This keeps our hearts right before God and our motivations pure.

Getting into the presence of God may be a little more complicated for some and for others not so much. I believe it all depends on your relationship with God. Are you immediately connected or distantly connected in fear of Him?

Do you remember your earthly Daddy? Were you able to talk over things with him or were you fearful of him because he was bigger and stronger than you?

Did you feel comfortable in his presence now and as a child? It all depends on the relationship? Know peace and this will change everything in a relationship.

What comes out of the presence? Let's talk about it here. It is only the great things:

Psalm 23:5
Thou preparest a table before me in the presence of mine enemies: thou anointest my head with oil; my cup runneth over.

Psalm 23 exudes the presence of God in every verse. David the shepherd of this Psalm had to guide and direct his sheep and he penned these beautiful words as he stayed in the presence of God. So much happens in the presence of God.

Psalm 16:11 broken down states in God's presence, these things happen:

1. We will get direction

2. We will get joy

3. We will find pleasures

This sounds like a treasure hunt and God has given us the keys to this treasure. They are not hidden but found in the Word of God.

Psalm 23:5 states we will find this in his presence:

1. We will be seated with our enemies at a table

2. Our Lord will anoint our heads with oil

3. Our cup will run over

Staying in God's presence brings with it great rewards and benefits. Deliverance is just one of them. But deliverance is so necessary in our walk with the Lord to get cleaned up so we can go up and be with the Lord in the sky and live with Him forever because He is a holy God.

As I look up the word presence in the Bible as in God's presence the Psalms are full of wisdom on the presence and I know David spent a lot of time in God's presence therefore called a man after God's own heart. God desires for us to be in His presence so we can have fellowship together.

Isaiah 64:1
Oh that thou wouldest rend the heavens, that thou wouldest come down, that the mountains might flow down at thy presence,

Isaiah 64:2
As when the melting fire burneth, the fire causeth the waters to boil, to make thy name known to thine adversaries, that the nations may tremble at thy presence!

Isaiah 64:3
When thou didst terrible things which we looked not for, thou camest down, the mountains flowed down at thy presence.

God's presence is necessary in my life because the Bible tells me that God lives in me when I got saved, so why should I ignore Him. He is my Savior. Isaiah says oh rend the heavens and come down... Come Lord Jesus come!!!

Rip open the heavens God and come to us! Even the mountains will flow in His presence. If God physically in His entirety stepped upon this Earth today, I am sure it would shake rattle and roll and tremble under His feet. But to be in His presence is an honor and a privilege never to be taken for granted.

I love when our Pastor speaks from the pulpit, *"Oh what a sweet presence of the Holy Spirit is here."* And he just *ous* and *ahs* until we finally start the service; our Pastor loves the presence of God and we love him for that.

God's presence automatically causes deliverance because He is a holy God. Some folks run out of services like that because they cannot stand the conviction or the fire of the presence. I have seen people leave. They cannot stand the holiness. Now I know they don't know why they are leaving offended but they gotta get out of there because their life does not line up with God's holy presence.

What does David say in the 51st Psalm?

Psalm 51:7 Purge me with hyssop, and I shall be clean: wash me, and I shall be whiter than snow.

8 Make me to hear joy and gladness; that the bones which thou hast broken may rejoice.

9 Hide thy face from my sins, and blot out all mine iniquities.

It doesn't ever say run away but get cleansed in the presence of God. Some are fearful to get right before the Lord but its better to do it here and now than to face it later in God's judgment. Deliverance is a necessary tool God uses to get his people cleaned up to serve Him in right standing before the Throne of Grace. Have you ever thought about that you (we all) are going to face Him one day and He is going to ask you:

"What did you do with that deliverance I sent your way?"

Now you stand before Him as filthy rags instead of cleansed by the Blood of the Lamb unto salvation because of why? Fear maybe or shame or guilt? We will all face Him in Heaven and we will all have to answer for much. Let's get deliverance today!

Genesis 45:7
And God sent me before you to preserve you a posterity in the earth, and to save your lives by a great deliverance.

God has been delivering his people since the Garden when Adam and Eve sinned. We as people were now born into sin and iniquity because of this royal first couple. So we need deliverance. But the presence of the Lord is the best deliverance you can ever receive and please do not go back to whatever you got deliverance from. Stay away and stay delivered. I have seen some folks who always go up front for prayer again and again because they cannot keep their healing or deliverance. God will not be mocked! What did Jesus say to the adulterous woman?

John 8:10
When Jesus had lifted up himself, and saw none but the woman, he said unto her, Woman, where are those thine accusers? Hath no man condemned thee?

John 8:11
She said, No man, Lord. And Jesus said unto her, Neither do I condemn thee: go, and sin no more.

STOP! Stop what you are doing; strive for holiness and righteousness in Christ Jesus! Give it all over to the Lord in prayer and supplication.

Psalm 40:13
Be pleased, O LORD, to deliver me: O LORD, make haste to help me.

LESSON # 3

DELIVERANCE

Your Will

Matthew 6:10
Thy kingdom come, Thy will be done in earth, as it is in heaven.

What is your will concerning deliverance? God never goes against our will. You must have a want to...

Let us keep praying that our will be God's will and that God's will be our will in everything we say and do. This may sound hard but we can pray so and say so and hope so, so shall it be, amen.

Matthew 25:21
His lord said unto him, Well done, thou good and faithful servant: thou hast been faithful over a few things, I will make thee ruler over many things: enter thou into the joy of thy lord.

We must align ourselves with God and our will is important to give over to Him, submit your will to God. How do we do this? Stay reading and studying the Word of God; stay in prayer and communication with Him and stay in a good Bible based church where iron sharpens iron.

What is a will? Defined by a dictionary is:

Will

[wil]

Noun

1. The faculty of conscious and especially of deliberate action; the power of control the mind has over its own actions: the freedom of the will.

2. Power of choosing one's own actions: to have a strong or a weak will.

3. The act or process of using or asserting one's choice; volition: My hands are obedient to my will.

4. Wish or desire: to submit against one's will.

5. Purpose or determination, often hearty or stubborn determination; willfulness: to have the will to succeed.

6. The wish or purpose as carried out, or to be carried out: to work one's will.

7. Disposition, whether good or ill, toward another.

God does not move against your will. You must want God; you must want salvation and you must want deliverance. Even David in his darkest hour repented and asked God to clean him up from all unrighteousness. (Psalm 51)

How can we ever move forward if we are carrying all those old things. That old baggage we carried from our world situation into our Godly situation? We have to give them up! We have to get delivered! When you love someone, don't you have to give up a lot? Marriage changes your life and you must begin to really share and if you don't you will have a guaranteed miserable marriage which will make for a miserable life. Life is full of give and take and when we come to the Lord we must give it over to Him. Give Him your bad habits, your nasty temper or your ugly addiction or your lust for others but give it over and get rid of it and hurry!!! God is waiting for you.

Matthew 16:26
For what is a man profited, if he shall gain the whole world, and lose his own soul? Or what shall a man give in exchange for his soul?

We can lose our souls or give it over to Jesus to perfect us, readying us for Heaven living eternally in God's presence. We talked about God's presence in the last chapter. So get up into His presence and give your will over to Jesus. It may sound hard but if you believe this is best for you, then it's easy. God does it! You offer it up.

Every day we learn more and more about how we should be and how our lives should be and how much we have missed out on because we were unable to give it over to the Lord. How long will you wait? How long will you carry that burden? God is good, and He has already provided the solution for you.

I remember coming to the Lord, when I was 46 years old; an old dog trying to learn new tricks? No, I was tired of my own mess and I wanted out of the repetitive errors and sin I was in. I was at the bottom of myself or the barrel you might say looking for the way out. Finally I got it! Jesus was my answer! Did it happen all right away you question? Oh no it took years and yet I am still learning and gleaning in others fields, sojourning through the mysteries of God. Has it been easy you ask? Oh no never but God has been so good to me at every fork in the road, he led me in paths of righteousness for His namesake as I prayed. (Psalm 23:3)

"Lord put me on your paths and not mine; paths of righteousness and not paths of destruction. Lord help me!"

I cried out in prayer and asked for God's help and He has helped me. He has picked me up many times; fed me and sustained me until I was rightly positioned in the Kingdom of God. We go from being babies to adulthood and there are many stages and in between that He has kept us on that straight and narrow path.

I learned to surrender to the Lord and it has been a journey. But you must surrender ALL: that three letter word that my husband loves so much because it is inclusive and saved a lot of time by saying: ALL. Trusting God with you and your things must be so in our walk with Him. TRUST is a big word! Do you trust God with your WILL? Then if your answer is yes just give it over to Him. Give it to Him now!

How do we do this? Give it all over to the Lord, speak it out in prayer:

Matthew 11:29
Take my yoke upon you, and learn of me; for I am meek and lowly in heart: and ye shall find rest unto your souls.

It is all an outward and an inward process and we must give it up and give it over to God. He has given us His only begotten Son hasn't he? Then we can give Him our will. He has given us His Holy Spirit, then our will is nothing in comparison, is it? Cleanse oh God cleanse us and purge us with hyssop until we give you our will fully.

God has given us free will, so let's freely give back:

Matthew 10:8
Heal the sick, cleanse the lepers, raise the dead, cast out devils: freely ye have received, freely give.

Romans 8:32
He that spared not his own Son, but delivered him up for us all, how shall he not with him also freely give us all things?

1 Corinthians 2:12
Now we have received, not the spirit of the world, but the spirit which is of God; that we might know the things that are freely given to us of God.

Revelation 21:6
And he said unto me, It is done. I am Alpha and Omega, the beginning and the end. I will give unto him that is athirst of the fountain of the water of life freely.

God has given us so much! From birth to death; from breath to life until we return to Him forevermore to be with Him, it will be a joy to surrender and be found in eternity.

Psalm 50:15
***And call upon me in the day of trouble:
I will deliver thee, and thou shalt
glorify me.***

LESSON # 4

DELIVERANCE

Your Heart

Romans 8:27
And he that searcheth the hearts knoweth what is the mind of the Spirit, because he maketh intercession for the saints according to the will of God

God needs your heart. There is where the blood flows in and out and keeps you alive every second of your day and night. If the heart is removed from our bodies then we would be a shell of a person with no life, period. God goes into our very life flow and knows your motive; your agenda; your sin and your thoughts because this heart should belong to Him. Everything happens because of the heart. Where is your heart today? Is it focused on Jesus? Or is it focused on your mess?

According to this above scripture God searches our hearts so He can make intercession for us. Yes Jesus prays for us. The heart must be kept free of any unnecessary gobblygook. The word that comes to mind is: *extraneous*.

Now that is God, I never use that word. Let's define it for mercies sake:

ex·tra·ne·ous

/ikˈstrānēəs/

adjective

- 1. irrelevant or unrelated to the subject being dealt with: "one is obliged to wade through many pages of **extraneous** material" synonyms irrelevant, immaterial, beside the point, not to the point, neither here nor there, nothing to do with it, not pertinent, not germane, not to the purpose, off the subject, unrelated, unconnected, inapposite, inappropriate, inapplicable, inconsequential, incidental, pointless, out of place, wide of the mark, peripheral, tangential antonyms material

What is in your heart? What is in the way of your moving forward? Is there something holding you back? Does it seem your blessings fade away or are slow in coming? What could this be?
What extraneous objects are blocking your blessings with the Lord?

1. Fear

2. Unhealthy relationships

3. Doubt and unbelief

4. A spirit of pride

5. A lack of patience

6. Unforgiveness

7. The ability to love

The heart is a significant organ and must be kept clean. It is the center of your living. I have a good friend in Karen L Sumrall and she teaches on Heart Throb Moments and she wrote a book on it and it is also a devotional and though there are many, many issues of the heart, it seems we never quite resolve them all. She seems to be flooded with the ideas and God keeps giving her more all the time. It seems she's tapped into the flow of God's heart. The heart can be messy business but we must get cleaned up so we can go up before the Father. Cleaned up so we can get into God's flow for our lives, knowing He loves us so and He is a preserver of life. His wisdom far exceeds ours of course.

People I know it's been said many times and I have said it in every book, these are the last days and God warns us about the perilous times coming. I believe we are already experiencing them and we must get our hearts cleaned up to go up! It's a big job with much yet to do.

Here is what the Bible says about your heart:

Proverbs 4:23
Keep thy heart with all diligence; for out of it are the issues of life.

This scripture says it all for me. It is bold in this warning. Out of your heart flow the issues of life. Of course without your heart there is no life. If you are not taking care of your heart which is probably the most important organ in your body, then you are not taking care of any other part of you. The old ticker as they used to call it is significant to keep your life flowing and going. Your blood, your DNA flows thru your heart as it keeps on pumping thru the rest of your systems and your organs. What else does the Bible say about your heart?

Luke 6:45
The good person out of the good treasure of the heart produces good, and the evil person out of evil treasure produces evil; for it is out of the abundance of the heart that the mouth speaks.

   There are many scriptures on the heart of man in the Bible as I saw as I searched for this scripture. There are many in this life today that have heart issues. What is in your heart? Your heart may need deliverance. Only our God can truly do that and do it well, because I know He did it for me, many times in my walk with Him. It is unfortunately very easy to carry unforgiveness in your heart for another. This must always go because otherwise it takes root and becomes bitterness. Oh this is not good! You can talk to a person a few minutes and know whether they have bitterness or not. You can hear it when they talk about what has happened to them. The indwelling of the Holy Spirit in you will catch it quickly by the tone of the voice speaking and of course the Holy Spirit knows all things.

   Your heart must be cleansed and free to do the work of the Lord. You cannot hide or deny anything wrong in your heart because God searches it and you cannot hide anything from God. But because He loves us so much, He wishes for all to be free of any harmful things in our hearts, that could ultimately destroy us.

3 John 1:2
Beloved, I wish above all things that thou mayest prosper and be in health, even as thy soul prospereth.

This is God's wish for us spoken plainly in the Book of 3 John. It's one of my favorites because it is so good what God wants for us. Please take care of your input and output of the heart. Some of these evil things held in the heart can cause blockages in life and come between you and God. Offense is one and do not take offense from or about another. Offense in the Body of Christ runs ramped and goes unchecked when someone takes it in because someone said something negative to or about you. SO WHAT!!! Don't take it in! Your heart cannot stand it! Get over it right away and forgive! Don't have a heart attack! Why should you take on offense when the person who said or caused it goes totally scott free? Well God will deal with them. You forgive them and pray for them immediately. Your job is to stay free not guard the other person's heart. But keep your own heart with all diligence. It is vital for living.

The blood is a whole another issue. The blood flows in and out of the heart which keeps you alive. Ask God to clean and purge everything in you, and repent for holding onto it this long. Turn from those ways and forgive others who have hurt you. I had to get deliverance from bitterness because I thought I had forgiven but went right back after I forgave and charged right back into that situation full-force, clean again. It really messed me up but turned into cancer which thank God He healed me of. But my own bull-headedness almost killed me and yes I am the one who loves Jesus so much! It could be you! Walk circumspectly. Let me give you two scriptures that remind me I can be fooled at times:

1. *Proverbs 26:11*
As a dog returns to his own vomit, So a fool repeats his folly.

2. *1 Peter 5:8*
Be sober, be vigilant; because your adversary the devil walks about like a roaring lion, seeking whom he may devour.

Be vigilant, amen.

* Footnote: Blessing blockers 1-5 is borrowed from Curt Landry's Ministry page online: One New Man Network on Spiritual Blessing Blocker. He has given us permission through simple text on his page. Thank you Curt Landry; now I receive all his e-mails. 6-7 was Holy Spirit derived from Susan J Perry the author of this book.

Psalm 18:49
***Therefore will I give thanks unto thee,
O Lord, among the heathen, and sing
praises unto thy name.***

LESSON # 5

DELIVERANCE

Thanksgiving

Thanksgiving sets you apart from the world and keeps you humble. Keeps your head low so your enemy can't see you and keeps us bowed before the Throne of Grace and at His feet to worship: the most high place! This is preventative medicine 101.

Oh my God! Thanksgiving is like the Wonder Woman of the Body of Christ. She fights crime in a most marvelous way and enters into God's Throne Room easily as Jesus waits and holds the door open just for you, like the gentleman He is. Why? Because you are so thankful! Some day either my husband or I am going to write a book on Thanksgiving. No not the holiday although it is one of my favorites. BOOM!!! Thanksgiving moves mountains and keeps one humble before God.

My husband and I begin thanking God in prayer before we go into the Throne Room because He has been so good to us. What does the Bible say?

Psalm 100:4
Enter into his gates with thanksgiving, and into his courts with praise: be thankful unto him, and bless his name.

What a beautiful creation in God this scripture is! It is perfect and it will get you in to see the King. You can get an audience before the King: the King of kings and the Lord of lords! God has given us the keys to His front door. He trusts us.

"JESUS! Thou Son of David, have mercy on me!"

Yes this will work too because it worked for the blind beggar on the streets while Jesus was leaving Jericho going towards Jerusalem. They screamed towards him to get his attention because they wanted their sight restored.

Matthew 20:30
And, behold, two blind men sitting by the way side, when they heard that Jesus passed by, cried out, saying, Have mercy on us, O Lord, thou son of David.

31 And the multitude rebuked them, because they should hold their peace: but they cried the more, saying, Have mercy on us, O Lord, thou son of David.

As Jesus passed by these men, he stopped and Jesus asked them a question of faith:

32 And Jesus stood still, and called them, and said, "What will ye that I shall do unto you?"

I always found this very interesting about Jesus; He often made a statement or asked a question before He healed most of the people. It wasn't that He was inquisitive; He being God already knew the answer before He asked but He checks on the faith of the one who needs the healing. Maybe they only wanted a cup of water or something to eat but no these beggars replied quickly and said:

33 They say unto him, "Lord, that our eyes may be opened."

This chapter 20 of Matthew is so good in, to describe the healing and deliverance nature of Jesus. He healed them all. We read that a lot throughout the New Testament about the ministry of Jesus. #1 priority is salvation, healing & deliverance. They are the powerful trio Jesus offers day to day for sinners who need him as well as the Body of Christ. What does Jesus do for these men? Here is what the next verse says:

34 So Jesus had compassion on them, and touched their eyes: and immediately their eyes received sight, and they followed him.

These men became followers of Jesus after being healed. Maybe that is what we need to do! Yell and scream and get the attention of Jesus:

"JESUS! Thou Son of David, have mercy on me!"

Well if you are lost and can't find your way or you are a prodigal and are backslidden then perhaps you need to yell and scream. Show Jesus your desperation! But for those of us who maintain a good relationship with Jesus throughout our days just:

"Enter his gates with thanksgiving and his courts with praise."

And you will gain entrance easily into the Kingdom of God remembering we always speak in the name of Jesus who is the door. It was written twice in the Book of John and I know God does not stutter but some times He must repeat himself to remind us of the truth.

John 10:7
Then said Jesus unto them again, Verily, verily, I say unto you, I am the door of the sheep.

John 10:9
I am the door: by me if any man enter in, he shall be saved, and shall go in and out, and find pasture.

   Enter in through the door. Enter in with thanksgiving in your heart. The King will receive you gladly. These are keys that unlock those big golden doors that gives you full access to the King in prayer and with intimacy.

   Thanksgiving will keep you delivered and close to your Abba Father. With thanksgiving you are lowly before the King and the enemy's arrows cannot get to you but go zing right over your head because you stay low. Thanksgiving brings you to the King in humility which is super key to come into God's presence. If you stay thankful, pride cannot enter in because you are thankful to God and not man. Pride is full of oneself and the ability to do it yourself. No, thanksgiving brings you closer to God when you acknowledge His deity and your dependence upon Him.

"Thank You Lord, I couldn't have done this without you!"

"Thank You Lord for this blessing!"

"Thank You Lord because You are sovereign and there is no other God but You!"

We have so much to be thankful for, now don't we? Can you think of a few things right now as you read? I can think of a kazillions of things to be thankful for. Get delivered of entitlement! There are so many people today addicted to this! Let me get the definition from Merriam Webster Dictionary for help so that you and I may understand more:

En·ti·tle·ment

/inˈtīdlmənt/

Noun

- *1. the fact of having a right to something: "full entitlement to fees and maintenance should be offered" synonyms right, prerogative, claim, title, license, permission, dispensation, privilege, liberty*

As children of God we often take for granted or think we are entitled because we are children of the Most High God. Get deliverance in this area if this is you! You can be saved and delivered in Jesus mighty name!

Get thee behind me satan! We must stay thankful knowing who our God is and who we are in Him. Think of that bloody cross and be thankful. We must never lose sight of the cross and all Jesus did for you and for me. It's a real big deal!

Do you remember how wonderful it was when you gave something or did something for someone else and they were thankful? It lightens one's heart. It's a good feeling to please another. God loves when we are thankful too, I am absolutely sure of it! He is ready to give us that next blessing!

We praise God with our thankfulness. He is worthy to be praised! He is great and greatly to be praised!

John 15:5
I am the vine; you are the branches. Whoever abides in me and I in him, he it is that bears much fruit, for apart from me you can do nothing."

P.S We wrote the book this year of 2020:
Thanksgiving is Best!
A Heart Full of Thanks Will Change Your Life!

1 Corinthians 10:16
The cup of blessing which we bless, is it not the communion of the blood of Christ? The bread which we break, is it not the communion of the body of Christ?

LESSON # 6

DELIVERANCE

Holy Communion

Jesus was delivered unto His destiny at the cross just after taking communion for the Passover meal. It was because He was the Passover Lamb who would give His life on the cross for all humanity. He knew no sin as we have, yet He gave His life for us. But He took communion first with His disciples. This was a very significant act on the part of Jesus because He came to earth to set an example for all of us.

Communion is a conduit for God's power and glory to be used mightily through this one simple obedient act. This is of God because it is named: Holy Communion. What did Jesus say before eating the bread and drinking the cup?

1 Corinthians 11:24-25
24 And when he had given thanks, he brake it, and said, Take, eat: this is my body, which is broken for you: this do in remembrance of me.

25 After the same manner also he took the cup, when he had supped, saying, this cup is the new testament in my blood: this do ye, as oft as ye drink it, in remembrance of me.

  This is a powerful tool in deliverance while doing communion as often as you like in remembrance of Jesus. Who can forget about what He has done on the cross and His life of miracles that produced so much love among the people. Let us do it in remembrance today.

  Communion is one of the tenets of the Church and if your church is missing this, than well there is an issue there. It's often use delivers and heals because of Jesus and His life given for us. There are many who call it the "meal that heals." So why are we missing it and the importance of it? Why as the church, the Body of Christ would we neglect this? It has made the Church sick and asleep. Take communion at home if you must.

  There have been many who have written the books on communion and yet the churches are shut down in 2020; the United States is full of Covid-19 and dying daily due to sickness and disease and our Lord and Savior provided the way out just before He died on the cross. People wake up and fly right!!! We must do as Jesus would have us do. Are we not called His followers? Are we not remembering Him as He asked on that prominent Passover Day?

  What is stopping you? Is it the power and suggestion of man? Go beyond that and take up the cup and the bread to honor Jesus. You will see a marked difference in your life, start today.

Psalm 28:2
Hear the voice of my supplications
When I cry to You, When I lift up my
hands toward Your holy sanctuary.

LESSON # 7

DELIVERANCE

Praise & Worship

Praise and worship always draws us closer to God as His presence envelopes us we are humbled and delivered. While in praise and worship you will be delivered and set free, just raise your hands to Jesus; lift up holy hands during this time and surrender yourself right here!

When a policeman catches a criminal he tells the prisoner to raise his hands in surrender. If we need deliverance, we are as prisoners and raising our hands in surrender to our God which is the beginning of deliverance knowing our God can do it. Deliverance of the believer becomes the business of our Almighty God who can do anything. Raise your hands in praise and worship. It will break all the fetters you have been tied up with. What happened to Silas and Paul in the prison? Their example is key to our freedom. We hear many preachers bring this word to the forefront in the Body of Christ because they need to hear it. Never stop praising God and worship brings you into the presence of our Daddy, our Father in Heaven. Our

Daddy is perfect, strong and mighty and He loves us intently. Many are not as comfortable with calling Him Daddy because of the fear of the Lord is the beginning of wisdom. I think it depends upon your relationship, just how close are you to the Father. Jesus sits at His right hand and He is both Son and Savior. Let Him set the captive free...

Acts 16:16-40

Paul and Silas in Prison

16 And it came to pass, as we went to prayer, a certain damsel possessed with a spirit of divination met us, which brought her masters much gain by soothsaying:

17 The same followed Paul and us, and cried, saying, These men are the servants of the most high God, which shew unto us the way of salvation.

18 And this did she many days. But Paul, being grieved, turned and said to the spirit, I command thee in the name of Jesus Christ to come out of her. And he came out the same hour.

19 And when her masters saw that the hope of their gains was gone, they caught Paul and Silas, and drew them into the marketplace unto the rulers,

20 And brought them to the magistrates, saying, These men, being Jews, do exceedingly trouble our city,

21 And teach customs, which are not lawful for us to receive, neither to observe, being Romans.

22 And the multitude rose up together against them: and the magistrates rent off their clothes, and commanded to beat them.

23 And when they had laid many stripes upon them, they cast them into prison, charging the jailor to keep them safely:

24 Who, having received such a charge, thrust them into the inner prison, and made their feet fast in the stocks.

25 And at midnight Paul and Silas prayed, and sang praises unto God: and the prisoners heard them.

26 And suddenly there was a great earthquake, so that the foundations of the prison were shaken: and immediately all the doors were opened, and every one's bands were loosed.

27 And the keeper of the prison awaking out of his sleep, and seeing the prison doors open, he drew out his sword, and would have killed himself, supposing that the prisoners had been fled.

28 But Paul cried with a loud voice, saying, Do thyself no harm: for we are all here.

29 Then he called for a light, and sprang in, and came trembling, and fell down before Paul and Silas,

30 And brought them out, and said, Sirs, what must I do to be saved?

31 And they said, Believe on the Lord Jesus Christ, and thou shalt be saved, and thy house.

32 And they spake unto him the word of the Lord, and to all that were in his house.

33 And he took them the same hour of the night, and washed their stripes; and was baptized, he and all his, straightway.

34 And when he had brought them into his house, he set meat before them, and rejoiced, believing in God with all his house.

35 And when it was day, the magistrates sent the serjeants, saying, Let those men go.

36 And the keeper of the prison told this saying to Paul, The magistrates have sent to let you go: now therefore depart, and go in peace.

37 But Paul said unto them, They have beaten us openly uncondemned, being Romans, and have cast us into prison; and now do they thrust us out privily? Nay verily; but let them come themselves and fetch us out.

38 And the serjeants told these words unto the magistrates: and they feared, when they heard that they were Romans.

39 And they came and besought them, and brought them out, and desired them to depart out of the city.

40 And they went out of the prison, and entered into the house of Lydia: and when they had seen the brethren, they comforted them, and departed.

The disciples and later the apostles went to prison for the preaching of the gospel. They were preaching freedom and the people imprisoned them for their faith. They didn't understand it and today if you look around it is still going on today. I know this is a big set of scriptures to read and study but they are so worth it for this chapter on praise and worship. Paul and Silas were supernaturally released from this prison thru their praise in the prison, beat and broken in chains they were, they lifted up a praise to God. Do you do that? Our God will set the captive free thru praise and worship in His holy name we pray and praise. He is our God who will see to your troubles whatever they are.

Today as I write this book I am facing a personal battle in my body and I know whom I serve and I trust He will free me once and for all no matter the weapon, it shall not prosper against me. (Isaiah 54:17) I lift my hands in praise and worship gladly because my sweet, sweet Jesus is going to do it!

Acts 16:25
And at midnight Paul and Silas prayed, and sang praises unto God: and the prisoners heard them.

God will come and get you in that midnight hour and correct all that has been done against you, God will restore and deliver you. In that last minute just before it's too late. God is right on time in every situation and if you stay in faith, He has marked you for the blessing. Deliverance is such a freedom from all that hinders you and I. Call upon Jesus today and He will hear you! He is where your help comes from!

Psalm 121:1
I will lift up mine eyes unto the hills, from whence cometh my help.

Proverbs 20:27
The spirit of a man is the lamp of the Lord, Searching all the inner depths of his heart.

LESSON # 8

DELIVERANCE

Inner Healing & Deliverance

Sometimes we must get at the root of things before we see healing and deliverance. Chapter #8 is New Beginnings for the believer, a new thing that God will do in you. It's on the inside that we must dig deeper and deeper. In the Book of Isaiah we go and we depend on God for these new things:

Isaiah 43:19
Behold, I will do a new thing; now it shall spring forth; shall ye not know it? I will even make a way in the wilderness, and rivers in the desert.

Matthew 9:17
Neither do men put new wine into old bottles: else the bottles break, and the wine runneth out, and the bottles perish: but they put new wine into new bottles, and both are preserved.

John 1:50
Jesus answered and said unto him, Because I said unto thee, I saw thee under the fig tree, believest thou? Thou shalt see greater things than these.

Jeremiah 33:3
Call unto me, and I will answer thee, and show thee great and mighty things, which thou knowest not.

God wants to show you things and you must get clean before He can do this. We must be a purified vessel because one day we will go be with Him as we are washed clean in the Blood of the Lamb, the Lamb of God who gave His Life, who gave His blood to cleanse us and set us free. He wants to take you to new places in Him but He can't with all that mess you got hanging around your neck, in your heart and in your soulical parts. We gotta ask God to cleanse us from all unrighteousness. David did and he got set free but unfortunately we still must pay the consequences of our sin. I don't see many books written about this, do you? I am going to check on this question while I am writing here...
I checked Amazon.com for my information and I did find a few books on it but certainly they are not very appetizing. Even deliverance does not give most folks a good taste in their mouths after the bitterness of their inner healing happens. I have had this happen and I know it does happen.

What is your bitterness about today? How are you reacting to certain subjects that go against the grain of your nature? Do you get easily angered? Do you cuss or get so upset it's like a pot being boiled? What happens in your life? That is the question we must all answer.

Do we take it out on our spouses; our children or our families and the Body of Christ? Where do you go for solace? Where do you take asylum from this enemy? There are so many things we are running from or running to? Take a look around your life and pray about it. It may be a profound moment in your lives as God defines the issues of your life...

Proverbs 4:23
Keep thy heart with all diligence; for out of it are the issues of life.

God wants to heal and deliver you of the regular bumps and bruises of every day life. There are a lot because you are not of this world but in this world that will beat you up literally just because you are you. Be healed and set free today...

In Jesus name all things are possible!

Your deliverance is always in God's hands and timing. This I know personally. But many illnesses and troubles are caused because we need inner healing and deliverance. If we look to the root of things, we usually see an inner cause. What happened in your childhood that hurt you? What happened when you lived with that man and committed secret sin? What is it you are hiding and it is affecting so much in your life negatively? Why, confess it to God, He knows it already and seek forgiveness from Him. We will never measure up to God's holiness but we need to take aim at that as a goal. Our inner hurts and wounds must be healed and delivered from anger, lust or hate, etc., etc. but we seek God for this. Some times you will run across a Preacher who knows how to reap deliverance through words of knowledge and the laying on of hands but all too frequently those folks are far and wide and the path is narrow to find them. They are rarely in your churches. My husband and I were trained under a very anointed deliverance Minister in the Florida area and we learned a lot. Jesus was one of those who cast out devils and healed their diseases and was not afraid to touch those who had leprosy in fear of catching it. Deliverance ministers are rare but when you find a good one, then grab ahold of the Hem of the Garment of Jesus because they are so valuable. I find them valuable!! The Body of Christ must find them valuable but often they find them offensive because they do the dirty jobs like the man of the Gadarenes, Jesus sought after the mighty storm in the boat. He overcame and delivered that monstrous man filled with many demons:

Luke 8:26-31

A Demon-Possessed Man Healed

26 Then they sailed to the country of the Gadarenes, which is opposite Galilee.

27 And when He stepped out on the land, there met Him a certain man from the city who had demons for a long time. And he wore no clothes, nor did he live in a house but in the tombs.

28 When he saw Jesus, he cried out, fell down before Him, and with a loud voice said, "What have I to do with You, Jesus, Son of the Most High God? I beg You, do not torment me!"

29 For He had commanded the unclean spirit to come out of the man. For it had often seized him, and he was kept under guard, bound with chains and shackles; and he broke the bonds and was driven by the demon into the wilderness.

30 Jesus asked him, saying, "What is your name?" And he said, "Legion," because many demons had entered him.

31 And they begged Him that He would not command them to go out into the abyss.

  Jesus delivered this man from every demon that tormented him inside and out. He has been trying to teach us but nobody wants that dirty assignment. So many stay demonized today and may never get set free. But it is my hope that through the power and presence of the Holy Spirit in one's life that will give us that overcoming power. (Revelation 12:11)

  Inner healing and deliverance is a delicate matter and most folks do not want it shouted out in a service for all to hear. It is often those secret places that carry the deepest hurts. Many times they are at the crux of your problem. This is where you dig deep into the problems and heartaches that you have experienced over a life time. Go to prayer, pray with others and dig, dig, dig until you find the root of a thing, then kill the root and get delivered. Here is what Jesus did:

Mark 11:12-25
Jesus Curses the Fig Tree

12 And on the morrow, when they were come from Bethany, he was hungry:

13 And seeing a fig tree afar off having leaves, he came, if haply he might find any thing thereon: and when he came to it, he found nothing but leaves; for the time of figs was not yet.

14 And Jesus answered and said unto it, No man eat fruit of thee hereafter for ever. And his disciples heard it.

15 And they come to Jerusalem: and Jesus went into the temple, and began to cast out them that sold and bought in the temple, and overthrew the tables of the moneychangers, and the seats of them that sold doves;

16 And would not suffer that any man should carry any vessel through the temple.

17 And he taught, saying unto them, Is it not written, My house shall be called of all nations the house of prayer? But ye have made it a den of thieves.

18 And the scribes and chief priests heard it, and sought how they might destroy him: for they feared him, because all the people was astonished at his doctrine.

19 And when even was come, he went out of the city.

20 And in the morning, as they passed by, they saw the fig tree dried up from the roots.

21 And Peter calling to remembrance saith unto him, Master, behold, the fig tree which thou cursedst is withered away.

22 And Jesus answering saith unto them, Have faith in God.

23 For verily I say unto you, That whosoever shall say unto this mountain, Be thou removed, and be thou cast into the sea; and shall not doubt in his heart, but shall believe that those things which he saith shall come to pass; he shall have whatsoever he saith.

24 Therefore I say unto you, What things soever ye desire, when ye pray, believe that ye receive them, and ye shall have them.

25 And when ye stand praying, forgive, if ye have ought against any: that your Father also which is in heaven may forgive you your trespasses.

    Jesus cursed the fig tree. He cursed it to the root and it died, it dried up miraculously. One day I was praying for someone and as I did I heard the Holy Spirit tell me to use these scriptures for cancer, to kill it at the root. It will dry up and produce no fruit. I have done this many times and had victory over the enemy of our souls. I am facing this battle today although I know the battle is already won because my husband cursed this foreign substance in my body and I know God dried it up at the root. And now I am believing for this miracle!

    Bitterness can cause much distress in a body, worry and anxiety but God will teach you via the Holy Spirit how to forgive; how to cast these negativities away in Jesus mighty name. They cannot stay with you if you are to be healed and set free, delivered of all. Earnestly set down with the Lord and give Him your heart to wash and cleanse. Sometimes He gives you a brand new heart for a fresh new beginning. He did this with me. I had ought against my brother and did not realize it but had to forgive him and set him free although it had been ten years since his death. God worked a real miracle in me through a dream in the night and I forgave and became whole again. It was not something I was even aware of until Jesus brought me the dream. When I spoke to the Lord casting all my burdens upon Him, He told me that He gave me a brand new heart. You know only God can do that. Stay faithful and thankful to God and He will change all your ways and deliver you from the snare of the fowler.

Psalm 91:3
Surely he shall deliver thee from the snare of the fowler, and from the noisome pestilence.

Psalm 91 is the greatest Psalm of reassurance from any kind of danger or sickness or whatever the world has to offer you. Get in the Bible and dig for your healing and deliverance. Psalm 91 is a great starting point.

The snare of the fowler today could be any snare of the enemy to hinder your walk with the Lord. Covid-19 comes to mind right away and all of its evil tentacles devised to bring this nation down and under subjection to evil forces out there but God has His plan and we are protected under the Blood of Jesus and all God has given us at the Cross. We carry special favor with God as angels camp round about us. Whom shall we fear?

Psalm 27:1
A Psalm of David. The LORD is my light and my salvation; whom shall I fear? The LORD is the strength of my life; of whom shall I be afraid?

John 8:32
And ye shall know the truth, and the truth shall make you free.

LESSON # 9

DELIVERANCE

Fear Must Go! Faith Must Come!

2 Timothy 1:7
For God hath not given us the spirit of fear; but of power, and of love, and of a sound mind.

God is concerned for your welfare, He therefore provides for all of your needs and fear is NOT a part of His provision ever, ever! Please do not be deceived by those who say that God makes us afraid. He never tries to scare us into a decision. The Holy Spirit is a gentleman who gently guides you into all truth. God does not need to persuade you through fear or intimidation and anyone who really knows God knows that His truth is straight up gospel! And this you may take to the bank! It will pay great dividends!

God's word is true and everyone who abides in Him knows this. Fear is man-made or devil made but it is not of God in anyway shape or form ever.

Fear is the opposite of faith. These two words oppose each other in every way. Let's define both of them here and now and you may see for yourself.

Fear

Noun

\ 'fir \

1a: an unpleasant often strong emotion caused by anticipation or awareness of danger
b(1) : an instance of this emotion

(2): a state marked by this emotion
2: anxious concern: solicitude

3: profound reverence and awe especially toward God

4: reason for alarm: danger

Verb

feared; fearing; fears

Transitive verb

1: to be afraid of : expect with alarm fear the worst

2: to have a reverential awe of fear God

3 archaic: frighten

4 archaic: to feel fear in (oneself)

Intransitive verb

: to be afraid or apprehensive feared for their lives feared to go out at night

Faith

plural faiths\ ˈfāths
, sometimes ˈfāt͟hz \

1a : allegiance to duty or a person : loyalty lost faith in the company's president
b(1) : fidelity to one's promises

(2) : sincerity of intentions acted in good faith
2a(1) : belief and trust in and loyalty to God
(2) : belief in the traditional doctrines of a religion

b(1) : firm belief in something for which there is no proof clinging to the faith that her missing son would one day return
(2) : complete trust

3: something that is believed especially with strong conviction especially: a system of religious beliefs the Protestant faith
on faith
: without question took everything he said *on faith*

Faith

Verb
\ ˈfāth

\faithed; faithing; faiths

Definition of *faith*

Transitive verb

archaic
: believe, trust

If you are afraid you are simply not in faith. Check yourself for this spirit. How are you handling your life? Are you walking in faith or operating in fear? That would be a first question. DO YOU TRUST GOD?

Are you a glass half empty person or a glass half full type person? Maybe we can dig a little deeper to see how you believe. It is important to check yourself.

How many times did Jesus say in the Bible: "O ye of little faith?"

1 Matthew 6:30
Wherefore, if God so clothe the grass of the field, which to day is, and to morrow is cast into the oven, shall he not much more clothe you, O ye of **little faith***?*

2 Matthew 8:26
And he saith unto them, Why are ye fearful, O ye of **little faith***? Then he arose, and rebuked the winds and the sea; and there was a great calm.*

3 Matthew 14:31
And immediately Jesus stretched forth his hand, and caught him, and said unto him, O thou of **little faith***, wherefore didst thou doubt?*

4 Matthew 16:8
*Which when Jesus perceived, he said unto them, O ye of **little faith**, why reason ye among yourselves, because ye have brought no bread?*

5 Luke 12:28
*If then God so clothe the grass, which is to day in the field, and to morrow is cast into the oven; how much more will he clothe you, O ye of **little faith**?*

6 Luke 19:17
*And he said unto him, Well, thou good servant: because thou hast been **faith**ful in a very **little**, have thou authority over ten cities.*

According to Bible Gateway my official online Bible resource it is 6 times. Make no mistake about the number six is the number God uses to denote man. God spoke through Jesus six times to man to have more faith and less fear! This whole exercise of six is important and has not been an exercise of futility because God always has a plan and a purpose and it's a good plan. (Jeremiah 29:11)

How many times did Jesus talk about great faith? This would be the opposite of little faith:

1 Matthew 8:10
*When Jesus heard it, he marvelled, and said to them that followed, Verily I say unto you, I have not found so **great faith**, no, not in Israel.*

2 Matthew 15:28
*Then Jesus answered and said unto her, O woman, **great** is thy **faith**: be it unto thee even as thou wilt.*

And her daughter was made whole from that very hour.

3 Luke 7:9
*When Jesus heard these things, he marvelled at him, and turned him about, and said unto the people that followed him, I say unto you, I have not found so **great faith**, no, not in Israel.*

This was only three times spoken that I can find stated this way although Jesus taught on faith, exercised faith and rejoiced when He saw faith in others. There is also a Gift of Faith which may be totally different here but you can surely seek God for it. We are given a measure of faith but the gift of faith is different.

Ephesians 2:8-9
8 For by grace are ye saved through faith; and that not of yourselves: it is the gift of God:

9 Not of works, lest any man should boast.

1 Corinthians 12: 8-11
8 For to one is given by the Spirit the word of wisdom; to another the word of knowledge by the same Spirit;

9 To another faith by the same Spirit; to another the gifts of healing by the same Spirit;

10 To another the working of miracles; to another prophecy; to another discerning of spirits; to another divers kinds of tongues; to another the interpretation of tongues:

11 But all these worketh that one and the selfsame Spirit, dividing to every man severally as he will.

These are spiritual gifts given to us by the Spirit of God.

What have you got to hold onto in these the last days? How did covid-19 affect your household? Did you grab a hold of your faith or allow fear to grip you instead? It's a pretty easy question that while we walk with God, these questions should be answered.

I inquired of my good friends **Frank & Karen Sumrall** to quote me the difference between faith and the Gift of faith because they have taught on the gifts many times and know exactly what I need to say here. Here is their quote:

Faith vs. Gift of Faith

Faith is given to every believer when they become born again. The Bible says it's a measure of faith! (Romans 12:3). It goes on to say God had dealt with us this measure that we should evaluate ourselves and not allow any pride to enter! Faith is an action we propel forward. It's a substance of reality by hope. I think TPT says it best:

"Now faith brings our hopes into reality and becomes the foundation needed to acquire the things we long for. It is all the evidence required to prove what is still unseen."
Hebrews 11:1 TPT

There are different degrees of faith that are needed in every believer at one point of our lives. Jesus described faith in people as He saw it: no faith, little faith, great faith. It seems the more we exercise our faith the more it increases! And we know without faith, it's impossible to please God! We can determine here, no faith being the measure of displeasing our Lord, while measuring great faith we would declare Jesus to be very pleased with that person!

The Gift of Faith is defined as just that: A Gift! The Holy Spirit wields this faith to whomever He wills. This gift is not measurable nor can it be exercised. When this gift is in operation, one will truly see ONLY God could have made the impossible possible. There is no question to mankind! You can't even imagine what the outcome would have looked like!

Frank & Karen Sumrall

P.S. Thanks to Frank & Karen Sumrall who have been given deep wells of wisdom and I am so thankful they allow us to tap into them every so often. It's such a blessing!!

Zechariah 13:9
I will bring the one-third through the fire,
Will refine them as silver is refined,
And test them as gold is tested.
They will call on My name,
And I will answer them.
I will say, 'This is My people';
And each one will say, 'The Lord is my God.' "

LESSON # 10

DELIVERANCE

The All Consuming Fire

Deuteronomy 4:24
For the Lord thy God is a consuming fire, even a jealous God.

Deuteronomy 9:3
Understand therefore this day, that the Lord thy God is he which goeth over before thee; as a consuming fire he shall destroy them, and he shall bring them down before thy face: so shalt thou drive them out, and destroy them quickly, as the Lord hath said unto thee.

Hebrews 12:29
For our God is a consuming fire.

Three times here the Bible speaks of God as a consuming fire. This to me is amazing! A fire will burn up the dross as we stand before God in the line of judgment removing all things not of God and worthless before Him. The fire delivers us and does a good job of it. It may hurt as you suppose because many things have been connected to us for a very long time. Deliverance ain't pretty.

God is Light and God is Fire and there is no illness, disease nor evil spirit that can stand before Him and live. There is none of this in Heaven where our God resides and as His children here on earth we cannot permit it to be near us as well but there are times when evil can tempt us, torment us and plague us in oh so many, many ways. We must be delivered from this. The Fire will burn it up in Jesus mighty name! I have felt this, I have known this and my experiences in the Fire of God have been plenteous! God has burned me up many, many times as He delivered me from the world, I submitted to the Fire.

God is so good and He knows exactly what we need. Right now as I am writing I can feel the embers of the fire in my belly rising up and it's so hot in there burning up my dross ready to touch others in these writings. Many times as I lay hands on the sick, they admit they can feel the fire. I have known the fire of healing and the fire of deliverance and although as young children we are taught to stay away from anything hot because it will burn you, the Fire of God is beneficial to all His believers. It burns up that which we do not need in our bodies; in our minds; in our wills and emotions. We must be set free! And I am thankful I have been there, glory to God! You can be too! Get under the umbrella of fire and feel it enclose around you like Meshach, Shadrach and Abednego and our God was the fourth man. Have no fear about it but have faith in the God who is the All Consuming Fire! He will deliver you from the heat, from the smoke and you will not be burned up but be cleansed by this enormous deliverance tool God utilizes.

These three men in the time of Daniel were eunuchs and God's men in the house of King Nebuchadnezzar who would not bow down to this kingdom and their idols and many of us know this story because it has been taught so many times from the Book of Daniel, chapter 3.

Daniel 3:22
Therefore because the king's commandment was urgent, and the furnace exceeding hot, the flames of the fire slew those men that took up Shadrach, Meshach, and Abednego.

Daniel 3:23
And these three men, Shadrach, Meshach, and Abednego, fell down bound into the midst of the burning fiery furnace.

Daniel 3:26
Then Nebuchadnezzar came near to the mouth of the burning fiery furnace, and spake, and said, Shadrach, Meshach, and Abednego, ye servants of the most high God, come forth, and come hither. Then Shadrach, Meshach, and Abednego, came forth of the midst of the fire.

Daniel 3:28
Then Nebuchadnezzar spake, and said, Blessed be the God of Shadrach, Meshach, and Abednego, who hath sent his angel, and delivered his servants that trusted in him, and have changed the king's word, and yielded their bodies, that they might not serve nor worship any god, except their own God.

Daniel 3:29
Therefore I make a decree, That every people, nation, and language, which speak any thing amiss against the God of Shadrach, Meshach, and Abednego, shall be cut in pieces, and their houses shall be made a dunghill: because there is no other God that can deliver after this sort.

Daniel 3:30
Then the king promoted Shadrach, Meshach, and Abednego, in the province of Babylon.

   As these scriptures show you the determination of these three brave men to serve our Almighty God, they were promoted after they survived the fiery furnace debacle. Look at God in verse 3:30: Let's repeat it:

 "Then the king promoted Shadrach, Meshach, and Abednego, in the province of Babylon."

   Promotion comes after the testing and the trials of fire because God is all up in it as was the fourth man in this fire for these three. We know that our Lord Jesus Christ was the fourth man in the fire protecting these dedicated God-fearing men. They didn't fear the fire, they became like the fire, their God who saved and delivered them from the wiles of their enemies. They succeeded because of their faith and courage in God. God delivered them by the fire. Here is the scripture introducing the fourth man:

Daniel 3:25
He answered and said, Lo, I see four men loose, walking in the midst of the fire, and they have no hurt; and the form of the fourth is like the Son of God.

We all walk out better for the fire cleanses us as pure gold burning out all the impurities which we do not see but often plague us. Oh no we serve a Mighty God!

I have been baptized in the fire of God and I have never ever been the same and neither will you!!! This is another aspect of the fire we need to touch on:

Matthew 3:11-12
11 I indeed baptize you with water unto repentance. But he that cometh after me is mightier than I, whose shoes I am not worthy to bear: he shall baptize you with the Holy Ghost, and with fire:

12 Whose fan is in his hand, and he will thoroughly purge his floor, and gather his wheat into the garner; but he will burn up the chaff with unquenchable fire.

This is God's will for His people. There is no other fire like the Fire of God who continuously burns us up in His beautiful presence. This scares many but He can burn up that fear as well because He is a consuming fire. Ask God for it. Do you remember the Israelites who sent Moses in their stead to stand before God on the mountain? But who did not live a good life because of their many fears, selfish wants and desires and pride kept them from God's fire but I believe it is better to seek God's fires rather than seeking the hellfires of satan, that dirty ole devil!! There is no comparison! What did the chosen people of God choose during Moses time up on the mountain? They melted their gold in the fire molding a golden calf for the people to worship in their minds of idolatry while substituting the Living God for a cow. Oh my, what is that saying about the faith of these people? Well none of them lived to see the Promised

Land. Do you want to live to see the Promised Land? I do; I want to see the Face of God and go up on the mountain as Moses did in his day and come back glowing for all to see.

Let's get fired up here on earth today! Let us get prepared and ask God for the Fire Baptism in Jesus mighty name! Seek Him and He will give it to you! He will deliver you into the hands of the Holy Ghost and Fire!

Malachi 3:2-3
2 But who may abide the day of his coming? And who shall stand when he appeareth? For he is like a refiner's fire, and like fullers' soap:

3 And he shall sit as a refiner and purifier of silver: and he shall purify the sons of Levi, and purge them as gold and silver, that they may offer unto the Lord an offering in righteousness.

Purge us oh God so we may be more like You!

God will refine you in His fire until you are as gold. (Zechariah 13:9)

James 4:7
***Submit yourselves therefore to God.
Resist the devil, and he will flee from
you.***

LESSON # 11

DELIVERANCE

Always Pray for Your Friends

Job 42:10-12

10 And the LORD turned the captivity of Job, when he prayed for his friends: also the LORD gave Job twice as much as he had before.

11 Then came there unto him all his brethren, and all his sisters, and all they that had been of his acquaintance before, and did eat bread with him in his house: and they bemoaned him, and comforted him over all the evil that the LORD had brought upon him: every man also gave him a piece of money, and every one an earring of gold.

12 So the LORD blessed the latter end of Job more than his beginning: for he had fourteen thousand sheep, and six thousand camels, and a thousand yoke of oxen, and a thousand she asses.

Job went through hell! Can anyone deny this? I surely cannot and I would not wish this trial on my worst enemy. Please know that Job knew God and his tests and trials were horrendous. As you read the Book of Job, and study Job you will find his experience excruciating to all who read and understand. Job lost everything but his life.

At one point in my life I tried to skip the Book of Job in my daily reading of the Bible because very often I felt like I had to live what I was reading. So I skipped it and started up in the Book of Psalms. I was not far in my reading and I heard a voice deep from within me saying,

"You know you will have to read Job!"

I groaned deep knowing this was the Holy Spirit speaking to me. As I nodded my head and agreed, I immediately went back and started with Job. It was a miracle knowing God watches over me this way. He watches over His word to perform it. You can bet on this. As a writer I know this truth very well. I write what God gives me as I am doing now knowing I must be trusted of God to do His will by the Spirit of the Living God.

We all must go through trials and tribulations in our walk with the Lord and there is nothing impossible with God. James speaks it best to count it all joy:

James 1:2-4
2 My brethren, count it all joy when ye fall into divers temptations;

3 Knowing this, that the trying of your faith worketh patience.

4 But let patience have her perfect work, that ye may be perfect and entire, wanting nothing.

   Job prayed for his friends. You know those friends who sat with him in his bed of affliction declaring doom and gloom over him, betraying him by the motivations of their hearts and the words of their mouth. 42 chapters later after all the misery Job suffered, he prayed for his friends. It took him a long time to get free enough to pray for others because of the mess he was in which seemingly blinded him. God chastised and rebuked him and woke him up spiritually so to speak.

Father God in Heaven please deliver us from unforgiveness and hurts that have been in our hearts about others. You always heal the broken-hearted; heal us today as we pray for our friends in Jesus mighty name!

   Job received double! Was it all worth it? Well Job lived a long time afterward. God satisfied Job and delivered him and restored his household; one that God could live with. Let God's will be done.

   As of this writing I have received a poor doctor's report, a sickness in my body and must face surgery in the next few weeks. I need to do this. God has been instructing me in oh so many ways. And before I even understood or knew it, the Lord put it in my heart to record a healing CD for others, so they might be delivered of their maladies, whatever they might be. Each of us has something kept hidden deep on the inside of us. Listen to the Holy Spirit and He will lead and guide you in everything. This Mother's Day, May 10th, 2020 we have sent out cards with CDS inside to touch others. I have gotten some really good feedback already. I pray friends get healed and delivered completely. It has been a test in my life that only obedience can rectify. We wrote a book also on healing titled:

**Heal Them All! The Children's Portion
Its available on Amazon.com in paperback and Kindle.**

I got a phone call from our Pastor the other morning and he asked me to give the Mother's Day message at church. I was amazed! I loved the idea of it! God is so good and when I asked Pastor if he was sure, he said yes I am sure, so I agreed. God started dealing with me right away in what I would be giving as a message. I have cards & healing CDs for all of the Mother's to hand out. I am excited about what God is doing in my life and the life of the folks around me and thankfully my husband stays supportive in so many beautiful ways. He is a gift from God! Our Church, our Pastor and family are a generous gift from God and I must stay thankful. Praise God!

What I am trying long and hard to say is deliverance comes when you pray for your friends. God in His reciprocal nature allows you to reap what you sow. If you need finances, pray for your friend's finances. If you need better health then pray for your friend's health issues. If you need love, sow love into your friends and family. Give what you need and you will receive it. This is an attribute of God. It is a basic principle that works in the Body of Christ and overall for that matter! Here is the confirming scripture:

Luke 6:38
Give, and it shall be given unto you; good measure, pressed down, and shaken together, and running over, shall men give into your bosom. For with the same measure that ye mete withal it shall be measured to you again.

This scripture represents so much in our walk with the Lord. This is how He gives to us and we should do as much or more with others. Be givers and not takers but receive the blessings of the Lord. It's not about money but the gifts of God to all of us!

Pray Without Ceasing Brings Deliverance

Acts 12:5-7

5 Peter therefore was kept in prison: but prayer was made without ceasing of the church unto God for him.

6 And when Herod would have brought him forth, the same night Peter was sleeping between two soldiers, bound with two chains: and the keepers before the door kept the prison.

7 And, behold, the angel of the Lord came upon him, and a light shined in the prison: and he smote Peter on the side, and raised him up, saying, Arise up quickly. And his chains fell off from his hands.

Prayer with God brings us into intimacy with God and intimacy with God brings deliverance. Look at Peter in these set of scriptures in the Book of Acts, a very supernatural beginning of the Church Age. Peter was in prison but the church was praying. Peter was in prison because he preached Jesus Christ and praying for him gave him freedom. Verse seven says the chains fell off of from his hands. Peter got set free from that prison that day. Then verses 8-9 say:

8 And the angel said unto him, Gird thyself, and bind on thy sandals. And so he did. And he saith unto him, Cast thy garment about thee, and follow me.

9 And he went out, and followed him; and wist not that it was true which was done by the angel; but thought he saw a vision.

   Through the prayers of the church God sent an angel to free Peter. God answers our prayers. We must not give up but continue to pray. And believe on God as we pray. Our hearts must be right before our God so our prayers will quickly come before Him and answered quickly to get the desired results. Then verses 10-12 gives more details of Peter's extrication:

10 When they were past the first and the second ward, they came unto the iron gate that leadeth unto the city; which opened to them of his own accord: and they went out, and passed on through one street; and forthwith the angel departed from him.

11 And when Peter was come to himself, he said, Now I know of a surety, that the LORD hath sent his angel, and hath delivered me out of the hand of Herod, and from all the expectation of the people of the Jews.

12 And when he had considered the thing, he came to the house of Mary the mother of John, whose surname was Mark; where many were gathered together praying.

Peter came to himself. He suddenly realized God was working on his behalf by sending an angel to aid him. God will send angels to be in charge over you! (Psalm 91:11) God is our help in time of trouble:

Psalm 9:9
The Lord also will be a refuge for the oppressed, a refuge in times of trouble.

Prayer will release the hand of God to help you. God cannot resist our cries for help, can He? Has He resisted you, ever? Can a Father resist the cries and needs of His children? No of course not, we have a good, good Father. We serve the Almighty God!!! He never turns His back on us. He said in the Word of God that He would never leave us nor forsake us.

1 Kings 8:57
The Lord our God be with us, as he was with our fathers: let him not leave us, nor forsake us:

Believe He is good and He will help you! Pray until something happens = P.U.S.H. This is the key for the believer.

1 Timothy 1:19-20

¹⁹ Holding faith, and a good conscience; which some having put away concerning faith have made shipwreck:

²⁰ Of whom is Hymenaeus and Alexander; whom I have delivered unto Satan, that they may learn not to blaspheme.

LESSON # 12

DELIVERANCE

Deliverance is Like a Shipwreck

Apostle Paul who traveled much, all over for the gospels of Jesus Christ teaching, preaching and writing the truth had a penchant towards shipwrecks. Here is the scripture that verifies this:

2 Corinthians 11:25-27

25 Thrice was I beaten with rods, once was I stoned, thrice I suffered shipwreck, a night and a day I have been in the deep;

26 In journeyings often, in perils of waters, in perils of robbers, in perils by mine own countrymen, in perils by the heathen, in perils in the city, in perils in the wilderness, in perils in the sea, in perils among false brethren;

27 In weariness and painfulness, in watchings often, in hunger and thirst, in fastings often, in cold and nakedness.

Thankfully Paul trusted God. Paul as Saul persecuted the Christians and the new church. He was a Pharisee until he had an encounter with the real, true and living God who was Jesus! Jesus delivered Saul that day as he fell to the ground and became blind to all sight. Saul became Paul and his life was changed in deliverance from the Old Man to the New Man in Christ Jesus our Savior. Before we get delivered we must know Christ as Savior!

Only God can deliver us, not man, not a doctor or a professor or any other layman. Only the Holy Man of Heaven can deliver you. And He will deliver us all one day, you will see this soon!

Paul traveled many times aboard ship to get to where God was sending him to preach the gospel and set up new churches. The waters must be traversed by the ships of that day. Often times the water was blown up by storms and tumultuous waves and we see this through out the times written about in the Bible. God can supersede the plans of the enemy even in the waters where there is great danger of death and destruction, God can calm the waves, save the people and deliver them to dry land. For nothing is impossible with our God! (Luke 1:37)

The ships of that day were fashioned and built in wood the only resource at that time were sometimes broken up in big storms out at sea. Paul says he was shipwrecked three times in 2 Corinthians 11:25. What a monumental miracle Paul received each time he was delivered alive from these paths of destruction meant to harm and kill him. Our enemy is always looking for ways to kill us and destroy the life God has given us. He wears us down hoping we will give up. But we cannot give up. Paul never gave up until that day he walked out to his death when they beheaded him by the sword of man, finally ending his days on earth. But Paul had eternal life as we do. No shipwreck could truly kill him because even today he lives eternally with Christ Jesus in Heaven where we will meet him one day. We will meet all those that have gone before us for this gospel of Jesus Christ and what an honor that shall be.

Our lives are constantly being rocked and rolled by these imps of satan who believes he will win the victory. Of course he will never win as we will see his reduction as he is cast into the Lake of Fire of hell forever and Jesus will reign sovereign forevermore. This job satan has is only temporary as are his temptations of sin.

"Get thee behind me satan!" Matthew 6:23

While we are shipwrecked God will deliver us onto dry land.

Exodus 14:29
But the children of Israel walked upon dry land in the midst of the sea; and the waters were a wall unto them on their right hand, and on their left.

God always delivers His people unto a safe and dry place for all to see the miraculous works of His hands. Can we shout right there?

"DELIVER US OH GOD TODAY!"

1 Corinthians 13:1

Love

1 I may be able to speak the languages of human beings and even of angels, but if I have no love, my speech is no more than a noisy gong or a clanging bell.

LESSON # 13

DELIVERANCE

The Heart of the Father is Love

Oh my Lord and Savior Jesus Christ there is no love like that which is in the heart of the Father. His love for us was and still is today a deliverer because He sent Jesus didn't He? How much love could He have had for us to deliver us from sin for all eternity...

John 3:16
For God so loved the world, that he gave his only begotten Son, that whosoever believeth in him should not perish, but have everlasting life.

What scripture could verify this truth any better? God the Father gave His Son for us who lived, died and resurrected on the third day and is now seated at the right hand of the father making intercession for all of us 24/7. Wow can you take this? It is an immense love our God has for us and for ALL humanity who often reject what He has to offer. Imagine God receiving this rejection day in and day out and that is why one of His attributes are long-suffering because this goes on and on until one day Jesus will come and retrieve us forever, His Bride.

Our deliverance comes when we love the Father in return through our salvation in Jesus Christ. Oh my God He is our deliverer every time and what can separate us from the love of God?

Romans 8:35-36

35 Who shall separate us from the love of Christ? Shall tribulation, or distress, or persecution, or famine, or nakedness, or peril, or sword?

36 As it is written, For thy sake we are killed all the day long; we are accounted as sheep for the slaughter.

One time I was praying in the car as my husband was driving us to a church meeting. I felt the presence of God as I prayed and asked to do whatever was in the Father's heart. I remember this was my request that evening. Suddenly I was inside of a huge bloody wall of a heart; I knew it was the Father's I must've been stopped with my mouth hanging open in awe is all I can say. I saw these walls I was inside of, the pleat in the skin and the dimpling of the surface. It had a bloody look to it and I knew my request was supernaturally answered that quickly. Suddenly when I realized what was happening I quickly came out of the vision or the actual visitation whichever it was only God knows and I began to describe it to my husband and he believed. It was so awe inspiring that it's hard to explain, I feel the presence of God as I try to explain right now on my body. He is here...

Jesus spoke in Matthew the truth we must all hear:

Matthew 22:37
Jesus said unto him, Thou shalt love the Lord thy God with all thy heart, and with all thy soul, and with all thy mind.

He loves us so much more and we can never fathom it or measure it but we can rely on it because He will deliver you every time! In His love there is freedom. He will give you salvation for eternity which has so many benefits for you and your family.

Psalm 97:10
Ye that love the Lord, hate evil: he preserveth the souls of his saints; he delivereth them out of the hand of the wicked

God as our Father keeps us from harm as harm tries to overtake us; instead He gave the task to Jesus to finish the job. There is no harm which can succeed against the Blood of our own beloved Jesus Christ. He is the extricator! He is the God who gave up His life to deliver us from all harm.

Psalm 145:20
The Lord preserveth all them that love him: but all the wicked will he destroy.

Love the Lord with all your heart. He wrote the Ten Commandments which I quoted in the Introduction of this book to keep us delivered because Moses climbed up that big mountain to go and get this from our Lord, twice. They must be important to our God who gave it to Moses twice!

Jesus tells it best again in the Book of Matthew which bears repeating again and again when asked by His disciples a very simple question:

Matthew 22:36-40

36 "Teacher, which is the greatest commandment in the Law?"

37 Jesus replied: "'Love the Lord your God with all your heart and with all your soul and with all your mind.'

38 This is the first and greatest commandment.

39 And the second is like it: 'Love your neighbor as yourself.'

40 All the Law and the Prophets hang on these two commandments."

How do we do this today? How is your heart as you read? Have you forgiven everyone in your past and in your generations? Do you hate anyone or hold onto bitterness about certain situations. Release them all now and give them all over to God, He loves you so much. He wants you delivered more than you want to be delivered. It is a good thing to cast it all at the feet of Jesus. Don't hang onto it but give it over: stress, anger, hate, unforgiveness, bitterness, envy or jealousy or any other negative feeling that is inside of your heart. Give it up! Jesus died for it all!

Our God's love is unchangeable, it is immeasurable, it is indestructible and it is unstoppable! There is none greater! He will always love you!

John 15:13
Greater love hath no man than this, that a man lay down his life for his friends.

   The Bible has a whole chapter written on God's Love in 1 Corinthians 13. Study it, know it and flow in it! The Love of God will deliver you!

   I can only speak from my own experience, I cannot speak from yours although I can quote you, I really do not know it. I can quote the Bible but until I experience it myself can I ever really know it. This I know. I was drawn to church because of the love that the congregation and its leaders showed me which led me to the love of the Father, Jesus Christ and salvation. When you receive Jesus into your heart, your heart changes in a process that is so filled with God's Love. Such a big love I had never known before and I suppose I will never know again. Only God can love us this way as He draws us. His Love is like the magnet of salvation. Then as I walked out my salvation, I wanted more and I asked for the indwelling of the Holy Spirit with the evidence of speaking in tongues which constitutes more and more love. When you truly love God you want all He has for you and more. Ask Him into your heart today and He will show you this love I am talking about because I have experienced this first hand!

1 John 1:7
But if we walk in the light, as he is in the light, we have fellowship one with another, and the blood of Jesus Christ his Son cleanseth us from all sin.

LESSON # 14

DELIVERANCE

Nothing But the Blood of Jesus

The blood of the Lamb will set you free. Jesus did everything on the cross including shedding His righteous blood for your deliverance.

"What can wash away your sin? Nothing but the blood of Jesus..."

This famous song is speaking of deliverance from sin, from our former life and it was all done on Calvary's Cross.

Revelation 1:5-6
5 And from Jesus Christ, who is the faithful witness, and the first begotten of the dead, and the prince of the kings of the earth. Unto him that loved us, and washed us from our sins in his own blood,

6 And hath made us kings and priests unto God and his Father; to him be glory and dominion for ever and ever. Amen.

God the Father delivers us by the blood of His very own Son who He put to death on that cross so we can live and be cleansed by all He did. The blood washes us clean. We cannot negate the cross if we are to be set free. The blood is the answer!

In the Old Testament they had to bring bulls, lambs and birds for offerings for sin and whatever else they required for a sacrifice to be killed on the Altar of God. It had to be a pure sacrifice and the animal's blood was a sign of cleansing and washing away of those sins. Today we have a new and better covenant, a blood covenant through Jesus Christ our Lord on the cross because He was considered a perfect lamb given for all mankind. The Book of Hebrews in the Bible speaks of this:

Hebrews 8:6
But now hath he obtained a more excellent ministry, by how much also he is the mediator of a better covenant, which was established upon better promises.

Hebrews 12:24
And to Jesus the mediator of the new covenant, and to the blood of sprinkling, that speaketh better things than that of Abel.

We are already walking in the victory when we accept Jesus Christ in salvation. Although it may be difficult for many to comprehend, the blood does it all! Read and study your Bible because Jesus was made the propitiation for our sins. Read Hebrews 9:11-28 of the Bible.

Romans 3:25-26

25 Whom God hath set forth to be a propitiation through faith in his blood, to declare his righteousness for the remission of sins that are past, through the forbearance of God;

26 To declare, I say, at this time his righteousness: that he might be just, and the justifier of him which believeth in Jesus.

What does propitiation mean? I know this is a big word for me too, let's define it right here:

pro·pi·ti·a·tion

/prəˌpiSHēˈāSHən/

Noun

- 1. the action of propitiating or appeasing a god, spirit, or person: "he lifted his hands in **propitiation**"

- 2. something that propitiates or appeases specifically**:** an atoning sacrifice, scapegoat.

My thought is that it is a substitution. In those days they often used a scapegoat to substitute for the actual whodunit. Jesus was used as a scapegoat for our sins which were dirty and shameful and yet we were cleansed and purged from His efforts on the cross. It is a difficult concept to grasp but when you know the Father, you understand the Son empowered by the Holy Spirit we are the benefactors of such a sacrifice.

Our lives are delivered and we are free to love again and know God.

Oh the blood, the blood of Jesus! There have been songs written; sermons preached and prayers said using the blood of Jesus. Jesus status and His blood is current. Just because Jesus died on the cross thousands of years ago, doesn't mean His blood today lacks power but it lives. The Bible says, *"The blood cries out!"* The blood still has life in it long after the body is long gone. And that's where they get the DNA from. The DNA of the blood continues to speak after you die.

Hebrews 12:24
to Jesus the Mediator of the new covenant, and to the blood of sprinkling that speaks better things than that of Abel.

Through the death of Jesus Christ, we are in blood covenant with God the Father in accepting Jesus Christ, His Son as Savior. It's in The blood where our covenant lies.

"Oh the Blood of Jesus! That washed away my sins, nothing but the Blood of Jesus!"

Many times when we are in the midst of a delivery service praying for someone, we cover them in the Blood of Jesus or we tell satan the Blood of Jesus is against you and the person gets set free. In the Blood of Jesus there are no obstacles but deliverance must come forthwith.

1 John 1:7
But if we walk in the light as He is in the light, we have fellowship with one another, and the blood of Jesus Christ His Son cleanses us from all sin.

Amen and amen.

Acts 2:21
And it shall come to pass, that whosoever shall call on the name of the Lord shall be saved.

LESSON # 15

DELIVERANCE

The Name of JESUS Will Deliver You!

The Blood and the name of Jesus are both synonymous with our freedom. The Body of Christ lives because of these two elements given to us by the Father of Heaven. My life is constantly being given over to deliverance because we are in this world but not of this world. (John 17:16) We must seek God for our deliverance but do it in the name of Jesus. We pray in the name; we believe in the name and we know in the name of Jesus!

The name of Jesus was set before the foundations of the earth I believe. God had it all planned out and man came along and messed it all up. But God always had a plan, He still does and it is for good and not evil so you many prosper and be in health. This name JESUS is above every other name and is more powerful than a locomotive, able to leap tall buildings in a single bound. No He is not Superman but He is Jesus who is above all. His name will deliver you!

Philippians 2:9-11

⁹ Wherefore God also hath highly exalted him, and given him a name which is above every name:

¹⁰ That at the name of Jesus every knee should bow, of things in heaven, and things in earth, and things under the earth;

¹¹ And that every tongue should confess that Jesus Christ is Lord, to the glory of God the Father.

    Everything and everyone will bow to the name of Jesus! You know I am reminded of a season when my husband and I were with a ministry that held our church services in a Jewish Temple. Oh what a time that was. God told us to enjoy the feasts and we were honored to even be there, a very holy place. God was enthroned in our praises. I will never forget this time, although a very religious setting we enjoyed our journey. Later the Temple was plagued by financial difficulties and they sold the building and we had to leave but today we still can remember it. But on the walls were plaques of many names who were honored in the Temple, those of Jewish faith and who had been faithful there to give and honor God. They had a beautiful tree on the wall of many gold nameplates of individuals who were frontiers in that area to this faith. It was so beautiful. As I often did, I would go before our service and peruse the names and dates and purposes for these name plates and it was then that I understood these set of verses in Philippians that I just quoted. The Jews do a lot of name plating on walls of synagogues and business offices because they are an honorable people. Then I saw by the Spirit of the Living God that the name of Jesus is above every other name and this is said because of their traditions and their values as a people. My Jesus is above every name whether it be of Hebrew, Arab or American descent, no matter because He is High and Lifted up and will draw all men unto Him.

Isaiah 6:1
In the year that king Uzziah died I saw also the Lord sitting upon a throne, high and lifted up, and his train filled the temple.

And

John 12:32
And I, if I be lifted up from the earth, will draw all men unto me.

What a beautiful thought this scripture brings to my heart and my thought processes...

God gives us such memorable experiences to draw from as we read scripture knowing that He is God! I love Him more for this!

I was in a church service long ago and as we were in praise and worship I looked up to see flashes of light up on the ceiling of the church building. I spoke to the Lord questioning Him by saying,

"Lord what was that?"

He replied, *"That is His train in the Temple."*

I was flabbergasted to say the least. I could not stop thanking Him. I was and still am so in awe of God. I got to see this scripture in real time today as I looked up there it was a white stream of light moving rapidly across my sight of vision. I want to tell you that I shall never forget this time in praise and worship! I loved it!! It is still as real to me today as it was then. God gives us memories that last to tell about in the years to come.

But because His name is above every other name in Heaven and on the Earth I got to witness that as well. I am a witness of how true the Word of God is. Some one said to me once that she does not take the whole Bible literally. Then I immediately disagreed and thought then you better watch out because some things in the Bible, do we really want to see or experience such as that of the life of Job? No not all but that which I have seen and experienced has been incredible. I take the whole Bible as truth and relevant for today's world as well as yesterdays. It is a literal book given to us for divine direction every day, in fact and not fiction and better to take heed of its instruction than to deny it. Woe to those who deny the power of the Word.

Timothy 3:1-5

1 This know also, that in the last days perilous times shall come.

2 For men shall be lovers of their own selves, covetous, boasters, proud, blasphemers, disobedient to parents, unthankful, unholy,

3 Without natural affection, trucebreakers, false accusers, incontinent, fierce, despisers of those that are good,

4 Traitors, heady, highminded, lovers of pleasures more than lovers of God;

5 Having a form of godliness, but denying the power thereof: from such turn away.

These are those perilous times today as I write and type on my computer it is Wednesday, May 13th, 2020. I know this scripture to be so true because we are living it. JESUS is a name we must believe on and use as a source of authority and power in our walk with the Lord and we shall be delivered and set free from all the chains that bind us.

Let us walk it out by faith and not by sight...
(2 Corinthians 5:7)

Proverbs 1:5-6
5 A wise man will hear and increase learning,
And a man of understanding will attain wise counsel,

6 To understand a proverb and an enigma,
The words of the wise and their riddles

LESSON # 16

DELIVERANCE

The Lesson on Counseling

Often times we need counseling in the Body of Christ one for another. Because we are not perfect nor ever will be until we get to Heaven to live with Jesus. We need each other's help. Find someone to speak to with whom you can trust. Look at their lives, check their heart's motivations and seek God for wise counsel.

Proverbs 19:20
Hear counsel, and receive instruction, that thou mayest be wise in thy latter end.

There are times when we truly need counsel and God's kind of wisdom. What does the Bible say about this?

James 1:5
If any of you lack wisdom, let him ask of God, that giveth to all men liberally, and upbraideth not; and it shall be given him.

There are always times to seek God for wisdom; to seek God for help and to seek God for the right person to speak with who can give you counsel by praying about it.

I remember we wrote a book titled: ASK for WISDOM: The Safe Harbor of God and was it a bestseller, well really I don't think so but it should have been. God gives wisdom and only God gives the true kind of wisdom. Man cannot get it any other place. I have written a few books and wisdom is still my favorite topic. Why you say? Well because God will give it liberally to those He deems as willing vessels. How did I qualify for wisdom? Surely I don't know the answer to this question but I love to go to God to get this hyperbole answered. His wisdom, the wisdom of God far exceeds anything I could ask or think. Wisdom is God's wheelhouse and I am trying to enter in through the door. I love wisdom; Jesus is the Spirit of Wisdom. If we love Jesus we must love wisdom. Is that true for you? Jesus is loaded with wisdom to be given away for all of those that seek Him.

Isaiah 11:2-4
2 And the spirit of the Lord shall rest upon him, the spirit of wisdom and understanding, the spirit of counsel and might, the spirit of knowledge and of the fear of the Lord;

3 And shall make him of quick understanding in the fear of the LORD: and he shall not judge after the sight of his eyes, neither reprove after the hearing of his ears:

4 But with righteousness shall he judge the poor, and reprove with equity for the meek of the earth: and he shall smite the earth: with the rod of his mouth, and with the breath of his lips shall he slay the wicked.

   Let's ask for wisdom and enter thru the door of God's wheelhouse finding out more and more. There are mysteries of revelation hidden away for all to find if you but seek the Lord. What has counseling and deliverance to do with all this wisdom, you ask? Well you need wisdom in order to help others and as we seek God for it, the more we receive. We surely do not only receive such things from God just for ourselves but to help others who perhaps have not gone that far in their walk with the Lord yet or trust enough to get this information themselves. Our gifts are always given to us for others. They are not solely for everyone but are for all you connect with and if they will listen to wise counsel.

   I often pray this for President Donald J. Trump that God would give him wise counsel. Just because none of us are an island unto ourselves; if so we will die alone and unwise. If we know God we just got bigger by one and then God begins to send others into our lives to help us along the way and angels come and help us as well. That is why we are known as the Body of Christ not just the children or the Lone Ranger of Christ and we must do it together to see the Light of God. God created it all this way, to stay together and work together to benefit many more than just ourselves.

Ecclesiastes 4:9-12
9 Two are better than one; because they have a good reward for their labour.

10 For if they fall, the one will lift up his fellow: but woe to him that is alone when he falleth; for he hath not another to help him up.

11 Again, if two lie together, then they have heat: but how can one be warm alone?

12 And if one prevail against him, two shall withstand him; and a threefold cord is not quickly broken.

In my early walk with the Lord when I was a single woman and I read these scriptures, meditated on them, it was like a light bulb suddenly came on. You know not everyone was born and raised in the church readily accepting the things of God. Although the Bible says precept upon precept and line upon line I knew I had to study because before I met the Lord I was blinded by my sin and deaf to the Word of God. So as I begun to read and study my eyes were no longer dim but opened slowly in God's timing and these set of scriptures made a big change in my thought patterns in that day. Suddenly I knew that I could not be alone, I longed for a husband and this three-strand cord they often spoke of being strong in the Lord together. We must do this life together!!

Counseling with others can bring deliverance. Wisdom can help you see the Light of Jesus removing the blinders on your eyes that the enemy put there for harm, God will turn it around for good, your benefit. This will be like a lesson learned that you will never forget. Let's try and define counsel for you:

Counsel

noun,

plural coun·sel for 3.
Advice; opinion or instruction given in directing the judgment or conduct of another.
Interchange of opinions as to future procedure; consultation; deliberation.

Verb (used with object), coun·seled, coun·sel·ing or (especially British) coun·selled, coun·sel·ling.
To give advice to; advise.
To urge the adoption of, as a course of action; recommend (a plan, policy, etc.): He counseled patience during the crisis.

Verb (used without object), coun·seled, coun·sel·ing or (especially British) coun·selled, coun·sel·ling.
To give counsel or advice.
To get or take counsel or advice.

   We often need advice so our walk with the Lord can have a firmly cemented foundation learning from others whose experiences are vast and knowledgeable in truth. Please be careful who you seek counsel with. But please ask God for discernment because a good friend could help you fall unknowingly. I have had friends to tell me things that could have led me astray and of course they had not meant to lead this way but I felt cautioned by the Holy Spirit although I did not always head the instruction, I went ahead regardless and I should have been more intent on what the Spirit was showing me. There are those of us that try to be a people-pleaser and that will bring about destruction in your life. Be a God-pleaser and learn from His instruction rather than man's. Always pray first and seek God! This is a good path; a sure path to victory.

One day I was really fed up with people and their actions and as I went into church my Pastor was headed right towards me in a big hug. I was so glad for that hug that day. The type that you would hope your Daddy would give you of peace and reassurance. That hug was good and as our embrace ended I said to my Pastor who is so lovely at the age of 82 today on May 11, 2020, "How do you put up with people?" Well he stepped back and more or less put on his wisdom cap and looked at me seeing my frustration and said, "Through the blood of Jesus." I looked at him and he said, "I asked the Lord a long time ago how do I cope with people?" "And the Lord answered me by saying, "Son see them as I see them, through the Blood of Jesus." "And when I started seeing folks that way everything was alright." He passed the wisdom of God along to me that day and it surely helps. I received wise-counsel.

When you love Jesus with an agape love like He loves us then the world seems bleak and dark and you often wonder why others act the way they do when they confess Jesus as the Lord of their lives but everyone's walk is different and we must know understanding with that revelation of wisdom. They belong together but it is all in God's timing such as this scripture which comes to my heart readily right now:

Ecclesiastes 3:11

11 He hath made every thing beautiful in his time: also he hath set the world in their heart, so that no man can find out the work that God maketh from the beginning to the end.

  God can take the ugliest some thing or some one and make them beautiful again. The world tears and rips up everything by all of its folly and self-centeredness but that's not our God. He is the Creator of Heaven and Earth and He can re-create and make every thing beautiful in His time. He will deliver many of us thru wise-counsel.

  I was delivered of frustration that day I inquired of my Pastor's wisdom and looking at people and their situations differently thru God's beautiful eyes and the Blood of Jesus who washes and sets the captive free. What a moment of remembrance that was for me, Thank you Lord, Thank you Pastor as we go through this life we must seek others and always seek God in prayer; His counsel is wisest of all. We have the Holy Spirit who teaches us all things on the inside of us, and we should be deeply appreciative for this God-given gift. There is wisdom and counsel in your belly, help to deliver others today!

  I had a dream this morning and I knew it was for the next chapter in this book. Dreams are an important part of our walk with the Lord. He gives us counsel in our night seasons and we are to write them down and I try to put some of mine in our books or at least the concept meant for them. My dream did not have real personal meaning except the fact that I was counseling others on the matters of life that were important to them. It seems God is giving me more opportunities to speak to others as I grow in the Lord and His wisdom far exceeds mine ever and He knows I pay attention to my dreams because my husband

and I pray for these every night that we pray together before sleep. So God supernaturally gives and I always know when they are from Him because they are colorful or vivid and memorable enough to tell my husband first. We try to dissect it and I get out my dream book if it's necessary but if its not and my understanding is full, I write it down and date it and thank the Lord for the fulfillment of this dream.

Counseling can bring deliverance freeing you from the menace of your own soul. Don't allow spirits to torment you or get your goat so to speak but seek counseling and seek the wisdom of God in prayer always. You will be in a much better place and peace will come.

Ask God in your prayer time to hear the voice of the Lord for yourself and He will counsel you personally and you will be delivered ultimately into His hands! Selah!

Psalm 16:7
I will bless the Lord who has given me counsel; My heart also instructs me in the night seasons.

Psalm 34:7
The angel of the Lord encampeth round about them that fear him, and delivereth them.

LESSON # 17

DELIVERANCE

Even the Angels Will Help You

I love receiving lessons from God, don't you? Yet here is another one for chapter 17; God gives angels charge over you (Psalm 91:11). Let's pursue this line of possibility for this new chapter.

Even Jesus as He prayed in the Garden of Gethsemane was ministered to by the angels as He sweated great drops of blood. God the Father sent His angels to help Him that day.

Luke 22:43
Now an angel from heaven appeared to Him, strengthening Him.

Before that in the wilderness as Jesus fasted for forty days and forty nights, God the Father sent Him ministering angels to keep Him from the temptation of the devil.

Matthew 4:11
Then the devil left Him; and behold, angels came and began to minister to Him.

Angels were sent the night that Jesus was born to tell of the *Good News* of His birth, that of our new Messiah.

Luke 2:10-12
But the angel said to them, "Do not be afraid; for behold, I bring you good news of great joy which will be for all the people; for today in the city of David there has been born for you a Savior, who is Christ the Lord. This will be a sign for you: you will find a baby wrapped in cloths and lying in a manger."

   These were messenger angels but they declared the *Good News* of Jesus Christ and we were glad. I am still glad about this news, A Savior was born to us this night.

   In the book of 1 Timothy there were witnessing angels and here it is stated so in scripture for you:

1 Timothy 3:16
By common confession, great is the mystery of godliness:
He who was revealed in the flesh,
Was vindicated in the Spirit,
Seen by angels,
Proclaimed among the nations,
Believed on in the world,
Taken up in glory.

And in Psalm 91 God sends angels to protect you and keep you safe:

Psalm 91:11-12
For He will give His angels charge concerning you,
To guard you in all your ways.
They will bear you up in their hands,
That you do not strike your foot against a stone.

God uses His angels for many purposes and in deliverance as you well can see is only one purpose. While Jesus prayed in the Garden of Gethsemane and sweated great droplets of blood, He obviously was suffering so much. Although it was exactly what He was meant to do, the angels came to His aid to strengthen Him. He was about to go to the Cross at Calvary and would give His life with a terrible beating and scourging to preempt His death beyond our mind's knowing and ability to endure. Humans are not meant for that kind of pain and destruction to endure before death. It was a horrible thing that Jesus endured for all of us! He died a very bloody and gory death before the people's eyes who witnessed it, should have been appalled with this brutality. But it seems man does not recognize the brutality with which it takes to murder another, therefore the Ten Commandments are key in our lives saying: 'Do not commit murder.'

That really should be a no-brainer for most. But today's society has lost the sensitivity towards the things of God as we see it every day on the news, on the television stories and movies. Hollywood glamorizes death and destruction every day it gets darker and darker and we as children of the Light cannot be involved in these things. They will bring you down into the pit of darkness with them. God will send His angels first before you go into darkness. You will receive many warnings and then He will send Jesus after you!

Matthew 18:12-13
12 How think ye? If a man have an hundred sheep, and one of them be gone astray, doth he not leave the ninety and nine, and goeth into the mountains, and seeketh that which is gone astray?

13 And if so be that he find it, verily I say unto you, he rejoiceth more of that sheep, than of the ninety and nine which went not astray.

There are many portraits of Jesus with a lamb slung over His strong shoulders carrying it back home to the fold. Don't get outside the fold. Jesus will come and get you all the while loving you and strengthening your walk with Him. It's a beautiful thing this walk with Jesus. But certainly God sends His angels to help you in many instances. God will draw us into safety always. He will never lead us into harms way to get us where we need to go. Thank God for the Father, the Son and the Holy Ghost who guide and direct us and send His angels charge over us as we go forth in strength and victory today.

We wrote a book about angels titled: Our Experiences With Angels by John R and Susan J Perry available on Amazon.com which helped me and our readers to learn more about the angels and how they operate. This I believe was a help to many as God guides me so deeply on every book and my husband had a vision while we prayed one night about how the angels stand next to me with these golden plates ready to give me information for these books. They help me to write and fill these pages as God sends them. The Word of God says:

Ezekiel 12:25
For I am the Lord: I will speak, and the word that I shall speak shall come to pass; it shall be no more prolonged: for in your days, O rebellious house, will I say the word, and will perform it, saith the Lord God.

God also says in the same Book of Ezekiel:

Ezekiel 37:14
And shall put my spirit in you, and ye shall live, and I shall place you in your own land: then shall ye know that I the Lord have spoken it, and performed it, saith the Lord.

God speaks through us and He watches over His word to perform it. It is His and whatever we speak or write we are held accountable for because of His Spirit in us. The Holy Spirit is involved all the time. We know that we know that God makes us stewards of everything we do for the Kingdom. Yes, God expects us to be good stewards of what He gives us to do. Each gift that stays unopened or unused or used improperly, I believe we will be held accountable for later on in the Bema Seat of Judgment. Yes we will be there and our works will be judged as either good works for the Kingdom or burn up as hay or stubble.

In the Book of Revelation, in chapter 22 it says:

12 And, behold, I come quickly; and my reward is with me, to give every man according as his work shall be.

13 I am Alpha and Omega, the beginning and the end, the first and the last.

14 Blessed are they that do his commandments, that they may have right to the tree of life, and may enter in through the gates into the city.
15 For without are dogs, and sorcerers, and whoremongers, and murderers, and idolaters, and whosoever loveth and maketh a lie.

16 I Jesus have sent mine angel to testify unto you these things in the churches. I am the root and the offspring of David, and the bright and morning star.

Here in these scriptures it says the Lord will give reward for our work. Jesus of course is our great reward. He is and always will be enough for me. Can no other reward you like Jesus! The Bema Seat is for the saints where we will receive our crowns and all our unnecessary works will be burnt up in the fire in heaven before our Lord. In verse 16 it talks about the angels sent to the churches to testify of our Lord Jesus Christ. Do you hear about Him in your church? Are you and your church rooted and grounded in the Lord Jesus Christ? I believe that is a question to seriously ask yourself in these the Last Days because the Bema Seat is graciously looming ahead of us to come and we will see it and we will participate in it and the angels will help guide us there so we won't miss a thing. Wouldn't want us to miss heaven would we? Now this is something we all need to consider and think and pray about. The question is not: Will heaven be ready for us but will we be ready for heaven and what is in store for us? We better get ready as we see the signs of the times and they are so perilous today. No not yesterday but today times are perilous and we see rapid change in the moral behavior of the world.

"Oh Come Lord Jesus come!"

John 15:19
If ye were of the world, the world would love his own: but because ye are not of the world, but I have chosen you out of the world, therefore the world hateth you.

LESSON # 18

DELIVERANCE

Deliverance From Worldliness

Look out churches because you must be on the right track with Jesus. Our lives must be right before Him. In the last chapter we spoke about angels and also the Bema Seat of Judgment in heaven and in this chapter I am going to tell you about the dream I had this morning pointing to the churches and how they are operating. Jesus turned over the money changer's tables because of the crooked commerce that was going on at the church. BEWARE these Last Days will bring even more tables turned over by the Lord if your church is operating in a worldly nature. God is not mocked. Look around and access your own church. Ask the question: Would Jesus be comfortable here? Or would He be comfortable in your home as well. We have Jesus everywhere in our home and I like to think He is comfortable.

So about my dream this morning; I feel like I am telling a friend because I have already told my husband and he is now off to work. The morning dreams I especially attribute to Jesus as I know that they are so real and cannot be quickly forgotten that when I am writing a book God gives me dreams and visions during that time. Let me repeat this scripture we used in chapter 16 on counseling:

Psalm 16:7
I will bless the Lord, who hath given me counsel: my reins also instruct me in the night seasons.

Various people in the Bible report of having dreams given by God. He gives us counsel while we are sleeping according to the above verse in Psalms. I love receiving from the Lord because it shows me His will for our book. The book is always dedicated to Him and for me it's a work I do for Him. He is my boss; He is my Father; He is my first husband and He is my All in All. He is absolutely everything to me.

1 Corinthians 15:28
And when all things shall be subdued unto him, then shall the Son also himself be subject unto him that put all things under him, that God may be all in all.

My dream: I was in a former church we used to go to years ago. My husband and I were together and we decided to go to the churches store to see what they had for purchase. It was in the front lobby of the church where you entered in the front doors. We went in and there was a very famous actress behind the counter at this store and they were filming a commercial with her as we stood by and watched. She was advertising the new church tee-shirts for sale and as she spoke she caressed her breasts in this commercial and it was very lustful in this sale of worldly items. And I was ready to bolt and the look on my face must have been one of fear or disgust I don't know but I felt as if I needed to run away because of the worldliness displayed in this church. And as she saw my face while the camera was running she lashed out at me with her words saying, "F.U." I am not going to spell this out for anyone. Because it will be an affront to God and the work He is doing here. I was shocked, right up in the church house. John and I were appalled and we walked right back out of the church. But it seemed no one else felt the same as we did, the camera man just kept right on filming as if this incident was nothing.

"Well I never!"

My dream ended with indignation and the thought of why is the Lord showing me these things? Then I remembered this book and how important deliverance from the world is upon salvation. When I got saved the process began as God started removing the world from my being and change was a process, a work was going on in me. Salvation is the most important step in this change. But this dream was as if the church was inviting the world in and accepting all it had to say and do. Yes the church is changing but changing for the worse and God was warning me and now I am warning you. Get out of that church if the world is running it, run and get out fast. What does the Bible say about this?

Revelation 3:13-16

13 He that hath an ear, let him hear what the Spirit saith unto the churches.

14 And unto the angel of the church of the Laodiceans write; These things saith the Amen, the faithful and true witness, the beginning of the creation of God;

15 I know thy works, that thou art neither cold nor hot: I would thou wert cold or hot.

16 "So then because thou art lukewarm, and neither cold nor hot, I will spue thee out of my mouth."

Oh my and this is talking about the Laodicean Church and speaks even louder in these next verses:

18 I counsel thee to buy of me gold tried in the fire, that thou mayest be rich; and white raiment, that thou mayest be clothed, and that the shame of thy nakedness do not appear; and anoint thine eyes with eyesalve, that thou mayest see.

19 As many as I love, I rebuke and chasten: be zealous therefore, and repent.

20 Behold, I stand at the door, and knock: if any man hear my voice, and open the door, I will come in to him, and will sup with him, and he with me.

21 To him that overcometh will I grant to sit with me in my throne, even as I also overcame, and am set down with my Father in his throne.

22 He that hath an ear, let him hear what the Spirit saith unto the churches.

Choose your church wisely just like anything else. Pray for direction from the Lord of lords and the King of kings who knows all and sees all. Keep the world of lust and other sinful spirits out of your precious church; your home and your life altogether. There is no place for this chaos and sin. We serve the Prince of Peace.

Oh my again who is on the Throne here? It must be the Lord Jesus Christ for the Church is His Bride and we must never forget that. How can she stay pure as a virgin ready for the wedding if she has brought the world into the church as in Jesus day? It seems nothing much has changed. Verse 22 says that we must listen to what the Spirit of the Lord is saying. This dream was a warning to the Church of today. And this Church I dreamed of is considered a mega-church and widely recognized throughout our country for its growth and the magnitude with which it was raised to this size. Be careful churches that you do not start mimicking the world in your content or bow down to their ways; their language or their lack of fear of the Lord. My God, my God I was ashamed and fear of the Lord overtook me even in my dream, I ran out quickly. Then as I got ready to get up in the morning, I chewed on the dream and realized that God was giving me another chapter for this book. It was shocking to me. Maybe I am old-fashioned but old-fashioned I'd rather be than be out of the good graces of my Father in Heaven. There will be terrible consequences for these churches who have compromised their walk with the Lord with the worldliness of the world. It will again create a mixture of ungodliness that will parallel those in the Bible who got out of the will of God. Please oh please not me my Lord come help us stay clean Lord Jesus!

The Lord very clearly states in the Word of God:

1 Peter 1:15-16

15 But as he which hath called you is holy, so be ye holy in all manner of conversation;

16 Because it is written, Be ye holy; for I am holy.

What is God's will for our lives? Do you really want to know?

"Be ye holy for I am holy."

That is God's will because it is in God's Holy Word and He is speaking to you and I today through dreams and visions and giving warnings because these days are before us and it is not long before Jesus returns. Get prepared Church; Get prepared the Body of Christ and get prepared world because our days are coming before the Lord!!

Romans 12:2
And be not conformed to this world: but be ye transformed by the renewing of your mind, that ye may prove what is that good, and acceptable, and perfect, will of God.

And

James 4:4
Ye adulterers and adulteresses, know ye not that the friendship of the world is enmity with God? Whosoever therefore will be a friend of the world is the enemy of God.

Be not of this world nor allow the world into your church so others conform to this world but let the world come in and be conformed to the things of God. Teach them, show them the way. We are going to be held accountable for these things and suddenly God has given me this burden to write about it and tell others and of course I will pray about it as well. It is big and it is devious how the evil ways of the world can be accepted in the churches. We are supposed to see change. It must be change that will change others in a good way.

"Be not conformed to this world!"

It is not a place the church should desire to be. We should desire to repent before God and ask forgiveness of our sins and ask for a cleansing of our hearts and souls before the *Return of Christ*. We must be washed clean to be His bride. I do not want to miss the great catching away of the saints. Do you? Does your church? Get some fire in your church in repentance, revival and restoration shall come to those who seek God diligently. Ask, seek and knock until you get true deliverance! It is urgent the Body of Christ get on their knees and pray until God changes your hearts. We cover you in prayer and in the Blood of Jesus Christ which brings deliverance. Oh the Blood, the Blood of Jesus makes us clean.

As I got out of the shower on the same day as I had the dream I began to pray for the churches to keep the things of the world out of them,

"Deliver them oh Lord in the mighty name of Jesus!"

And the Lord brought to my memory Achan in Joshua 7 who had stolen some things from Jericho after their victory and God told Joshua about it after the defeat at Ai.

18 Finally, Joshua brought each man in Zabdi's family to the L<small>ORD</small>, and the L<small>ORD</small> showed that Achan was the guilty one.

19 "Achan," Joshua said, "the L<small>ORD</small> God of Israel has decided that you are guilty. Is this true? Tell me what you did, and don't try to hide anything."

20 "It's true," Achan answered. "I sinned and disobeyed the L<small>ORD</small> God of Israel.

21-22 While we were in Jericho, I saw a beautiful Babylonian robe, two hundred pieces of silver, and a gold bar that weighed the same as fifty pieces of gold. I wanted them for myself, so I took them. I dug a hole under my tent and hid the silver, the gold, and the robe."

Joshua had some people run to Achan's tent, where they found the silver, the gold, and the robe.

23 They brought them back and put them in front of the sacred chest, so Joshua and the rest of the Israelites could see them.

24 Then everyone took Achan and the things he had stolen to Trouble Valley.[a] They also took along his sons and daughters, his cattle, donkeys, and sheep, his tent, and everything else that belonged to him.

25 Joshua said, "Achan, you caused us a lot of trouble. Now the L<small>ORD</small> is paying you back with the same kind of trouble."

The people of Israel then stoned to death Achan and his family. They made a fire and burned the bodies, together with what Achan had stolen, and all his possessions.

26 They covered the remains with a big pile of rocks, which is still there. Then the LORD stopped being angry with Israel.

That's how the place came to be called Trouble Valley.

Achan and his whole family were put to death. This is how the Lord thinks of His Bride and the world. Church do not steal the things of the world and contaminate the Bride of the Church because she belongs to Jesus and not to you but He has given it to you to steward and care for. What kind of job have you done? Are you in trouble with the Lord today? The church must repent and get right before the Lord.

Then He brought to my memory Rachel who was given her husband Jacob and while leaving her father's household stole his idols or gods that did not belong to her but her father. God was involved in Rachel's life, why did she steal these idols?

Genesis 31:34
Now Rachel had taken the images, and put them in the camel's saddle, and sat upon them. And Laban searched all the tent, but found them not.

What was her need? What was the purpose of this incident that God is bringing back to me now? Rachel is a picture of the church today. Although we serve the Living God and He is with us, we drag in the idols of the world contaminating the purity of the Church. Jesus wants a pure church without spot or wrinkle. God is about to purge His Bride from all contamination, from all worldly possessions and change the face of the church before man messed it up with his fleshly ways of the natural.

  Pray Church Pray... Repent Church Repent... Restore God Restore...

IN JESUS NAME!

Ephesians 5:27
That he might present it to himself a glorious church, not having spot, or wrinkle, or any such thing; but that it should be holy and without blemish.

  Deliverance is needed in the church for the church body. We gotta kick the world out and all of its associates pertaining to wealth and riches by ill-gotten gain. This is not of the church but God the Father will provide for His Son's Bride completely. And He will never provide the things of the world to entertain the church. We must be so careful! Seek God if you are in any doubt and He will give you all the answers. The contamination must be delivered in Jesus name!

Mark 1:32-34

32 And at even, when the sun did set, they brought unto him all that were diseased, and them that were possessed with devils.

33 And all the city was gathered together at the door.

34 And he healed many that were sick of divers diseases, and cast out many devils; and suffered not the devils to speak, because they knew him.

LESSON # 19

DELIVERANCE

Demons, Devils and Deliverances

What a scary proposition this is for many of God's people today. The secrets finally come out as well as the demons and devils that try to hide amongst you all but cannot hide from Jesus and all His plans and purposes. No devil you must come out in the name of Jesus! Many people shrink back from any dealings with this kind of deliverance:

#1 It ain't pretty!

#2 It can be messy!

#3 It can be a long drawn out process!

#4 You cannot do it in the flesh but must be empowered by the Spirit!

What does the Bible say about this? Jesus healed them all? Aren't we supposed to do this too? Aren't we supposed to do greater things?

John 1:48-50

48 Nathanael saith unto him, Whence knowest thou me? Jesus answered and said unto him, Before that Philip called thee, when thou wast under the fig tree, I saw thee.

49 Nathanael answered and saith unto him, Rabbi, thou art the Son of God; thou art the King of Israel.

50 Jesus answered and said unto him, Because I said unto thee, I saw thee under the fig tree, believest thou? Thou shalt see greater things than these.

   Jesus spoke this over us in explanation to others and so shall it be unto us. We need to receive whatever Jesus spoke. We all need to be deliverance ministers one way or another. The people need to be free from any bondage that holds them captive of the enemy of their souls. Most cannot live this way because of a bondage that will take over your life creating chaos and trouble and must be delivered before the suffering gets so deep it becomes more difficult. Get to the root right away and cast it out! As we covered before: in Jesus name we cast it out and get deliverance.

Matthew 8:28
And when he was come to the other side into the country of the Gergesenes, there met him two possessed with devils, coming out of the tombs, exceeding fierce, so that no man might pass by that way.

   Here was a man with many devils and His name was Legion because of the number of devils who possessed him. Jesus cast them all out and sent them into the swine that ran over the cliff and perished. The man was a raging, naked demoniac before the Lord. Some times you got to get naked before God and give Him all your dirty little truths so He can set you free from all of this. Only Jesus could do this! Man would have been killed under this demonic oppression! There are many types of deliverances and this was one of the heavy-duty ones that required the strength and power of the Lord. If we tried this and we had only one tiny little hair out of place that man could have jumped on us, killed us and walked off like nothing happened. As deeply as possessed as this man was of these devils he probably had no conscience left at all. The Bible calls it a seared conscience.

1 Timothy 4:1-3

1 Now the Spirit speaketh expressly, that in the latter times some shall depart from the faith, giving heed to seducing spirits, and doctrines of devils;

2 Speaking lies in hypocrisy; having their conscience seared with a hot iron;

3 Forbidding to marry, and commanding to abstain from meats, which God hath created to be received with thanksgiving of them which believe and know the truth.

We must seek God in all things. We must be prayed up and delivered ourselves if we are to do like Jesus did and walk in His power to deliver. This was a major task for Jesus; although we are not to be afraid of these encounters but do we have enough stuffing on the inside of us to get such a big job done? The deliverance ministers I know live a fasted and prayerful life because the Bible says it this way:

Matthew 17:21
Howbeit this kind goeth not out but by prayer and fasting.

This is a lifestyle with which ministers of deliverance live by so their lives are strong as God governs their actions to win these battles. We must be more than conquerors, overcomers by the Blood of the Lamb and the word of our testimony as in Revelation 12:11.

Jesus must needs go through Samaria (God is just giving this to me now):

John 4:4 And he must needs go through Samaria."

Jesus always went out of His way to heal and deliver the people because the needs were great! The Samaritan Woman at the Well of Jacob was one candidate for deliverance because she had had five husbands and the one she was living with was not her husband. She needed to be set free of her bondages of sin. She received the Living Waters of Jesus during their famous conversation and became the first fervent woman evangelist to be known of in Bible times. She went about telling all men.

John 4:28-30

28 The woman then left her waterpot, and went her way into the city, and saith to the men,

29 Come, see a man, which told me all things that ever I did: is not this the Christ?

30 Then they went out of the city, and came unto him.

  Jesus delivered them all with the words to set them free and by the powerful anointing He carried and used this one little woman coming late to the well to draw some water. He gave her the Living Waters of Christ! She then spread those waters throughout her territory, telling all. Telling others about Jesus is a necessary part of our deliverance in giving glory to God for all He has done, never taking credit by man but only by The Father, The Son and The Holy Ghost who now live on the inside of us to set others free. What does the Bible say about this? Let me give you my living scripture which is right on for this time and message:

Revelation 12:11
And they overcame him by the blood of the Lamb and by the word of their testimony, and they did not love their lives to the death.

  My testimony will help you get delivered because it is truth between me and Jesus who is the Living God who will give you the Living Waters also. I have seen sooty demons come out of me as a former smoker and I was set free thru a massive deliverance, many years ago. I am sure I have already told the story in this book somewhere. Commanding the devils to get out is not an option but must be commanded in Jesus mighty name! They cannot stay because as a Christian, it is illegal territory for them. The only time is when you open the door thru sin to allow them to come in and make their abode. Oh no, no, no don't do that. Quickly ask for forgiveness and repent before the Lord to remove access of the enemy. After the enemy has left you, go in unto the Lord in prayer seeking His guidance and cover yourself, your life in the Blood of Jesus sealing your deliverance.

DO NOT OPEN ANY DOORS TO THE ENEMY!

What does the Bible say?

James 4:7

Humility Cures Worldliness

Therefore submit to God. Resist the devil and he will flee from you.

This scripture makes it real and easy for the people of God's Kingdom; resist only. So let's do some resisting today and seek God for a better way. He must deliver you, clean you up and be your Lord 24/7. Are you ready for this type of deliverance? Sometimes reality can be harsh. Now stay on God's narrow path, so you will not have to suffer the devil all the time.

Matthew 7:13-14

The Narrow Way

"Enter by the narrow gate; for wide is the gate and broad is the way that leads to destruction, and there are many who go in by it. Because narrow is the gate and difficult is the way which leads to life, and there are few who find it."

Psalm 34:17
The righteous cry, and the Lord heareth, and delivereth them out of all their troubles.

LESSON # 20

DELIVERANCE

Killing the Fruit of Cancer

Matthew 21:18-22

18 Now in the morning as he returned into the city, he hungered.

19 And when he saw a fig tree in the way, he came to it, and found nothing thereon, but leaves only, and said unto it, Let no fruit grow on thee henceforward for ever. And presently the fig tree withered away.

20 And when the disciples saw it, they marvelled, saying, How soon is the fig tree withered away!

21 Jesus answered and said unto them, Verily I say unto you, If ye have faith, and doubt not, ye shall not only do this which is done to the fig tree, but also if ye shall say unto this mountain, Be thou removed, and be thou cast into the sea; it shall be done.

22 And all things, whatsoever ye shall ask in prayer, believing, ye shall receive.

  Our God is such a good, good Father and I know you have heard this song before as sung in our churches and radio stations, etc. he takes good care of His children. Whatever the devil meant for harm, the Lord will turn it around for good! I trust God!

  These scriptures of when Jesus cursed the fig tree are the ones God gave me when praying for others especially for those with cancer. It is an important revelation because when Jesus cursed this tree, it died from the root up killing everything about it and it would never bear fruit under the direction of Jesus because His words were more powerful than a double-edged sword and I for one believe this option is good. Isn't this what they try to do with radiation and chemotherapy when they blast our bodies with it trying to kill the cancer which grows and spreads? Makes sense doesn't it?

When just reading these scripture verses over again out loud I realized that Jesus spoke words of faith to get the job done. When you pray and ask; when you pray and declare a thing or decree you must have your faith in line with your words so that you will see action. So your words become action promptly.

See what verse 20 says that the disciples saw it and they marveled how quickly this fig tree withered up. Our words must be strong and full of faith in order to work for others as we pray for them. They have to hit the bulls-eye of the target so illness will dry up and become as powder quickly blown away by the desert winds.

Cancer especially has the characteristics of spreading and that's why we must dry it up at the roots so there will be no spread of the disease. Invasive diseases in our bodies have roots and that root must die in order to be healed in Jesus mighty name! Now another root may be addressed at this time: cancer as well as other diseases often are caused by things like unforgiveness; bitterness, hatred and grievous other heart attitudes. Ask Jesus to check your heart to reveal the cause of any obnoxious sickness or disease which could cause a malady plaguing your body. Jesus says we must forgive all. Who is holding onto your health heart-strings for you? Question thyself and question the Lord in prayer. He will always help you!

Recently I have had a dangerous diagnosis and I will have to go through the surgery as the Lord told me so to go ahead and get r'done! I knew that I knew that I would be on assignment for Jesus at the doctor's offices and the hospital. I will be speaking for Him. Do I want to or like this prospect of my walk with Jesus, well NO! But I want to be obedient to my Lord and Savior! I know His plans and purposes are far bigger than mine and His perspective is far reaching with the big picture of Panavision. I always believe that Jesus has a wide-angled camera much bigger and wider than anything I could have seen or photographed. Maybe that's a silly way of thinking but don't forget His names and attributes are:

Revelation 22:13
I am Alpha and Omega, the beginning and the end, the first and the last.

I know Jesus is sovereign and He will always have the final say in my health and in yours. Some times it's just that person's time to go to Heaven and no prayers can stop the inevitable. But we try regardless. Praying should always be an option we choose for others. Our bodies break down as we age, perfect health seldom occurs here on earth. Have you ever seen this? It's in our choices isn't it?

We see so much of this in our society today: health foods; health clubs; fitness and exercise; diets that starve the better of you and sickness such as bulimia and anorexia and other addictive behaviors because our society promotes skinny. Skinny is not pretty folks and it is certainly not healthy. We see runway models, actors and actresses dying prematurely by starving themselves or by enhancing their lives with artificial means of available drugs. Sports figures enhance their performances with drugs and die unnecessarily

because of the need for speed or keeping their weight down to perform. God did not make us this way. But man has so perverted God's creation because they now have the artificial means to so. Do you think God is pleased by this? No one can love God and do this. Are we not the Temple of the Holy Spirit? Are we acting accordingly? Have we become a godless society worshiping idols, our bodies and man rather than the God who has created it all! We need to repent before God for those things that can kill us!
Check out this scripture:

1 Timothy 4:8
For bodily exercise profits a little, but godliness is profitable for all things, having promise of the life that now is and of that which is to come.

How can we ignore what scripture says? Our lives depend upon it to exercise our hearts for Jesus as we believe it says here. Hallelujah! That can give you cause to shout right there!

Prayer saves! Praise and worship saves! Intimacy with God saves! Jesus saves and not man! Please reconsider your relationship with the Lord and have Him search your heart! He will show you your deficit and save you from early death, and you could be this recipient of life more abundant as it says in the Word of God:

John 10:10
The thief cometh not, but for to steal, and to kill, and to destroy: I am come that they might have life, and that they might have it more abundantly.

This scripture verse says it all. Satan comes to kill us giving us detrimental ways to kill us physically as well as spiritually but Jesus says He came to give us life and life more abundantly. We need life these days which are so perilous, God watches over His Word to perform it. I believe I have quoted this before but realize sometimes we must repeat ourselves to bring this to our remembrance because it is important for your life too. Cancer or no other disease has a right to be in your body, you are a child of the Most High God and healing and deliverance is said to be the children's bread. Jesus died for our healing. Jesus gave us His wholeness or Zoë life as is mentioned in John 10:10. This is a pure life offered by our God because Jesus lived free of sin; free of sickness and disease and free from any lack of any good things, so do we receive this upon salvation from the Lord Jesus Christ? It is our portion! It is given freely by the Savior! Deliverance from any worldly negative should be easy when we know Jesus. Jesus is free then so should we be. What does the Bible say throughout the scriptures?

Matthew 8:22
But Jesus said unto him, **Follow me***; and let the dead bury their dead.*

Matthew 9:9
And as Jesus passed forth from thence, he saw a man, named Matthew, sitting at the receipt of custom: and he saith unto him, **Follow me***. And he arose, and* ***followed*** *him.*

Follow me...

This is the best solution to all of our daily woes, follow Jesus into your Promised Land; into your healing and deliverance and into your freedom forevermore...

Amen.

TESTIMONY

Approximately in March of this year of 2020 I was diagnosed with colon cancer and when I had inquired of the Lord, He let me know it had to be taken out. So He found me the right surgeon and the right hospital (the best) which took really good care of me. Of course we had been praying and seeking God about this cancer issue many times over. My family had it over and over and we thought we had broken that generational curse too. (All part of deliverance 101).

People had seen the tumors or polyps as they are called when praying for me several times and I was a little bit wary but we kept on believing and we kept on praying. Our church was praying, our friends were praying and still we had to go into the hospital and have an operation. It was very successful and I praise God for it. We met several wonderful nurses and my doctor was so good I almost felt like he was my brother. I was honored to give out some of our books while there as thank yous to those who were so good to me. I prayed for them earnestly and the entire hospital.

The disease came even though we prayed against this disease for others almost every day. Did we do something wrong in our walk with the Lord, maybe but what could we have done differently. I honestly do not know but I do know that my God is always good and we give Him all the honor and the glory and try to keep walking upright.

Psalm 84:11
For the Lord God is a sun and shield: the Lord will give grace and glory: no good thing will he withhold from them that walk uprightly.

I am still believing I will never walk this way again, I inquired of the Lord through this time and He said, *"This was a test."* Do I understand it, NO, but maybe on the other side of Heaven it will be revealed. I chose to be joyful in the Lord but I must admit I had an opportunity to feel grumpy at times because often times the prognosis isn't good for cancer but I serve a God who is able to do more than I can ask or think. The one nurse at the hospital gave me the "Gold Star Award" for being the best patient of the day. I was so surprised. Friends sent flowers, their love and prayers and I knew there were angels all around aiding me. So I was in good hands. In two days they were able to send me home and the following day, today I am here typing this out so somebody can get set free with the Love of God! The devil is a liar, never forget that obvious fact!

I really don't have time to suffer but I will be careful and rest because God has given me His rest but I got things to do, people to see and places to go. The miracle of God is available for every believer. Get jiggy with it!

Isaiah 63:14
As a beast goeth down into the valley, the Spirit of the Lord caused him to rest: so didst thou lead thy people, to make thyself a glorious name.

June 3, 2020

PS After coming home from the hospital I struggled with a very few things but God let me know since I had surgery and the doctors had me all opened up and working on me that some doors had been opened and that my husband John would need to anoint my head, pray over me and as the head of our household (this is key) close all the open doors that now existed. He closed the trauma door; he closed the cancer door; he closed the infirmity door and opened me up to divine health and strength. Involuntarily I felt a deep breath of air push out of my lungs and I coughed. I got deliverance. Strange as it may seem, I felt at peace again and my husband seemed relieved to help me. It is key to have the head of your household help you. If you don't have one then seek your Pastor or an elder of your church, perhaps someone you really trust. Here is the scriptures I am standing on today as I look back over these past few months and all that has gone on, this is my home base, this is where I want to hang my proverbial hat:

Philippians 4:11-13

11 Not that I speak in respect of want: for I have learned, in whatsoever state I am, therewith to be content.

12 I know both how to be abased, and I know how to abound: every where and in all things I am instructed both to be full and to be hungry, both to abound and to suffer need.

13 I can do all things through Christ which strengtheneth me.

My 2 final testimonial scriptures came as the Lord spoke to my heart which is now all apart of my new testimony of healing and deliverance. Here they are:

1. Psalm 30:2 O LORD my God, I cried out to You, And You healed me.

2. Nahum 1:9 What do you conspire against the LORD?
He will make an utter end of it.
Affliction will not rise up a second time.

2 Samuel 22:2
And he said, The LORD is my rock, and my fortress, and my deliverer.

LESSON # 21

DELIVERANCE

Deliverance From Bullies

BULLY DREAM
July 29th, 2020

I was lying in a bed with the covers on; I remember a blue blanket over me, lying on white sheets. I was awake but waiting for something. This big buff guy comes along, very muscular and with his shirt off showing his very large muscles and physique which did not impress me at all! And then tries to seduce me to go along with him and I say no. Suddenly he sits on top of me holding me down by his strong body weight, he tried to bully & coerce me into being with him; accepting him and his ways. I kept telling him no and to get off of me. He was a big bully, much bigger than me and finally he gave in and got off of me and left me totally alone there in the bed. When I awoke from this dream I was disgusted although it was not sexual at all. I did not succumb to this bully! I knew this bully and it was cancer. I got the victory!

James 4:7
Submit yourselves therefore to God. Resist the devil, and he will flee

There are many bullies in this life if we look around or look back at our lives and the lives of others. I recently battled the bully of cancer but I knew that if I waited on the Lord and stayed of good courage that I would get the victory! And we did.

Remember David and Goliath one of the most victorious stories in the Bible about defeating one's enemies when they look bigger than you can handle. No way little David (in stature) could handle that giant of Goliath's stature of over 9 feet tall; so it is speculated of his size in that day. Consider 5'1" or so in David's youthful size in comparison to over 9' in the giant's size which would cause anyone to run and run away fast. David accepted the task at hand from God and went to the brook and picked up 5 smooth stones to use in his sling against the giant, because he had brothers too. David went prepared. David had no fear because he knew God was in this and He knew whom he served. We must know that we know at any given time.

All the other men around him and the armies of that day including his own brothers had mocked and chastised him in this matter. Who do you think you are David, you half-pint you? I am sure much laughter broke out in the camp mocking David's abilities! But they were surely caught unawares when David defeated this big enemy who threatened them all. (Study 1 Samuel 17) While David speaking here to Saul the King:

1 Samuel 17:
36 Thy servant slew both the lion and the bear: and this uncircumcised Philistine shall be as one of them, seeing he hath defied the armies of the living God.

37 David said moreover, The Lord that delivered me out of the paw of the lion, and out of the paw of the bear, he will deliver me out of the hand of this Philistine. And Saul said unto David, Go, and the Lord be with thee.

38 And Saul armed David with his armour, and he put an helmet of brass upon his head; also he armed him with a coat of mail.

39 And David girded his sword upon his armour, and he assayed to go; for he had not proved it. And David said unto Saul, I cannot go with these; for I have not proved them. And David put them off him.

40 And he took his staff in his hand, and chose him five smooth stones out of the brook, and put them in a shepherd's bag which he had, even in a scrip; and his sling was in his hand: and he drew near to the Philistine.

41 And the Philistine came on and drew near unto David; and the man that bare the shield went before him.

42 And when the Philistine looked about, and saw David, he disdained him: for he was but a youth, and ruddy, and of a fair countenance.

43 And the Philistine said unto David, Am I a dog, that thou comest to me with staves? And the Philistine cursed David by his gods.

44 And the Philistine said to David, Come to me, and I will give thy flesh unto the fowls of the air, and to the beasts of the field.

45 Then said David to the Philistine, Thou comest to me with a sword, and with a spear, and with a shield: but I come to thee in the name of the Lord of hosts, the God of the armies of Israel, whom thou hast defied.

46 This day will the Lord deliver thee into mine hand; and I will smite thee, and take thine head from thee; and I will give the carcases of the host of the Philistines this day unto the fowls of the air, and to the wild beasts of the earth; that all the earth may know that there is a God in Israel.

47 And all this assembly shall know that the Lord saveth not with sword and spear: for the battle is the Lord's, and he will give you into our hands.

48 And it came to pass, when the Philistine arose, and came, and drew nigh to meet David, that David hastened, and ran toward the army to meet the Philistine.

49 And David put his hand in his bag, and took thence a stone, and slang it, and smote the Philistine in his forehead, that the stone sunk into his forehead; and he fell upon his face to the earth.

50 So David prevailed over the Philistine with a sling and with a stone, and smote the Philistine, and slew him; but there was no sword in the hand of David.

David then grabbed the huge sword of Goliath and cut his head off for a trophy to take away to prove the victory of man over beast. This is a story we all know and love. We have heard it since we were little children but it is a good one for our every day lives. We battle bullies every day as we get sick; as we go to work; as we watch the news and hear what is going on in this world today! God is about to get rid of your bullies, do not succumb to their power! Yes they may be physically stronger than you but you are spiritually stronger because of your life in Jesus and He conquered all on the cross. He defeated death, hell and the grave so what are you afraid of?

CRY OUT, "JESUS!"

And surely He will come running! He will defeat your bullies because He told me once He will SUPERSEDE all the plans of the enemy! He will always give us the victory and deliver you from the bullies playing around your school yard. You can remember them. Maybe it was you who was the bully at that time, then repent before God today and ask Him to forgive you. He will you know! Maybe it was you who used to run away and cry because of the bully hiding behind your mother's or your teacher's skirts. Those young days were tough! We were learning. They say David was only seventeen when he killed that giant, not quite a man yet. But because God gave him the strength to do this and it is a feat that will always be remembered through the annals of time or until Jesus comes to get us, we get these victories too.

Praise God the victory is ours!

1 Corinthians 15:57
But thanks be to God, which giveth us the victory through our Lord Jesus Christ.

PS We recently contracted covid unawares but while our church is suffering unfortunately, I know we are not afraid. Covid is just another bully the devil has sent out to cause fear to grow in people. But as we know Jesus we know we will pass this test too. This year of 2020 has been filled with its tests and willingly or unwillingly we set those bullies aside and worship the Lord Jesus Christ because of His love and mercy for us which are renewed daily. We have much to be thankful for. Glory to God!

2 Peter 2:9
The Lord knoweth how to deliver the godly out of temptations, and to reserve the unjust unto the day of judgment to be punished.

LESSON # 22

DELIVERANCE

Whomsoever

God has laid it upon my heart often that He never goes against man's will. He gives us all the opportunity to be delivered and set free but as He has said to me and is printed on the front page of this book:

"You must have a want to!"

God keeps giving this new lesson by its one-word title: Whomsoever.
He will do it for all of us but we must seek Him and ask for this deliverance. He knows exactly what you need and why you keep getting into trouble; or why you can't seem to get out of a bad situation; be healed or why your relationships all turn sour, etc., etc. There are many needs for deliverance today. But God wants you to know that your needs are special and He wants to tend them but first you must always have a want to for yourself. Speak out loud:

"Help me oh Lord!"

God will always help you in any case. He sent the Holy Spirit to us because He is: The Helper and the Comforter for life.

I sought out Bible scripture about this one word title of WHOMSOEVER and I found 20 scriptures in the KJV and let's look at them here to see what they reveal:

Genesis 31:32
*With **whomsoever** thou findest thy gods, let him not live: before our brethren discern thou what is thine with me, and take it to thee. For Jacob knew not that Rachel had stolen them.*

Genesis 44:9
*With **whomsoever** of thy servants it be found, both let him die, and we also will be my lord's bondmen.*

Leviticus 15:11
*And **whomsoever** he toucheth that hath the issue, and hath not rinsed his hands in water, he shall wash his clothes, and bathe himself in water, and be unclean until the even.*

Judges 7:4
*And the Lord said unto Gideon, The people are yet too many; bring them down unto the water, and I will try them for thee there: and it shall be, that of whom I say unto thee, This shall go with thee, the same shall go with thee; and of **whomsoever** I say unto thee, This shall not go with thee, the same shall not go.*

Judges 11:24
Wilt not thou possess that which Chemosh thy god giveth thee to possess? So **whomsoever** *the Lord our God shall drive out from before us, them will we possess.*

Daniel 4:17
This matter is by the decree of the watchers, and the demand by the word of the holy ones: to the intent that the living may know that the most High ruleth in the kingdom of men, and giveth it to **whomsoever** *he will, and setteth up over it the basest of men.*

Daniel 4:25
That they shall drive thee from men, and thy dwelling shall be with the beasts of the field, and they shall make thee to eat grass as oxen, and they shall wet thee with the dew of heaven, and seven times shall pass over thee, till thou know that the most High ruleth in the kingdom of men, and giveth it to **whomsoever** *he will.*

Daniel 4:32
And they shall drive thee from men, and thy dwelling shall be with the beasts of the field: they shall make thee to eat grass as oxen, and seven times shall pass over thee, until thou know that the most High ruleth in the kingdom of men, and giveth it to **whomsoever** *he will.*

Daniel 5:21
And he was driven from the sons of men; and his heart was made like the beasts, and his dwelling was with the wild asses: they fed him with grass like oxen, and his body was wet with the dew of heaven; till he knew that the most high God ruled in the

kingdom of men, and that he appointeth over it **whomsoever** *he will.*

Matthew 11:27
All things are delivered unto me of my Father: and no man knoweth the Son, but the Father; neither knoweth any man the Father, save the Son, and he to **whomsoever** *the Son will reveal him.*

Matthew 21:44
And whosoever shall fall on this stone shall be broken: but on **whomsoever** *it shall fall, it will grind him to powder.*

Matthew 26:48
Now he that betrayed him gave them a sign, saying, **Whomsoever** *I shall kiss, that same is he: hold him fast.*

Mark 14:44
And he that betrayed him had given them a token, saying, **Whomsoever** *I shall kiss, that same is he; take him, and lead him away safely.*

Mark 15:6
Now at that feast he released unto them one prisoner, **whomsoever** *they desired.*

Luke 4:6
And the devil said unto him, All this power will I give thee, and the glory of them: for that is delivered unto me; and to **whomsoever** *I will I give it.*

Luke 12:48
But he that knew not, and did commit things worthy of stripes, shall be beaten with few stripes. For unto

whomsoever *much is given, of him shall be much required: and to whom men have committed much, of him they will ask the more.*

Luke 20:18
*Whosoever shall fall upon that stone shall be broken; but on **whomsoever** it shall fall, it will grind him to powder.*

John 13:20
*Verily, verily, I say unto you, He that receiveth **whomsoever** I send receiveth me; and he that receiveth me receiveth him that sent me.*

Acts 8:19
*Saying, Give me also this power, that on **whomsoever** I lay hands, he may receive the Holy Ghost.*

1 Corinthians 16:3
*And when I come, **whomsoever** ye shall approve by your letters, them will I send to bring your liberality unto Jerusalem.*

Let us define the word whomsoever, a word not very commonly used in today's language. We need a clear understanding to expound:

whom·so·ev·er

/ho͞osō'evər/

relative

- 1. used instead of "whosoever" as the object of a verb or preposition: formal "they supported his right to marry **whomsoever** he chose"

OR

whosoever
[hoo-soh-ev-er]

pronoun; possessive whose·so·ev·er; objective whom·so·ev·er.

1. whoever; whatever person: Whosoever wants to apply should write to the bureau.

Our God is no respecter of persons; He loves and wants what's best for us all. Deliverance is part of that deal because if you want to be close to God the Father, God the Son and God the Holy Spirit then we need to become more and more like Him every day and in every way. So get delivered today in Jesus mighty name, Amen.

1 Peter 1:15-16
But as he which hath called you is holy, so be ye holy in all manner of conversation;

Because it is written, Be ye holy; for I am holy.

Genesis 45:7
And God sent me before you to preserve you a posterity in the earth, and to save your lives by a great deliverance.

LESSON # 23

A Reprieve

As I prayed about the book this morning knowing it is almost at its end readying for publishing, I had a quickening in my spirit to seek the Lord about this topic. Deliverance can be very messy business and usually when I write something, I must also live it. Just like the Prophet who prophesies and the Pastor who guides the sheep and the sent one of the Apostles and the Evangelists who capture the hearts of the sinners with Jesus as well as the Teacher who teaches the Word of God; we must be accountable. We seek the Lord and He answers and this morning of December 22, 2020 at approximately 7:17 AM, I heard: ***"A Reprieve!"***

This sounded good to my ears as I prayed and heard the word of the Lord and I pray we will ALL hear this word together. We need a reprieve at this time during our holidays getting ready to go into 2021 which promises that God is sovereign and still in control although many have fallen away this year and forgotten this big truth. Our God is The Sovereign God; The Almighty God and there is no other and of this fact alone I can promise you, He is!

Let's look at the word reprieve and see what it means for us today:

re·prieve

/rəˈprēv/

Verb

- 1. cancel or postpone the punishment of (someone, especially someone condemned to death): "under the new regime, prisoners under sentence of death were **reprieved**" synonyms grant a stay of execution to, cancel/postpone/commute/remit someone's punishment, pardon, spare, acquit, charge, punish

Noun

- 1. a cancellation or postponement of a punishment: "he accepted the death sentence and refused to appeal for a **reprieve**"

God is granting us a reprieve today. No punishment is necessary but deliverance will still be an unavoidable process to live clean and healthy before God. Come on we all need it in some way. We all have fallen short of the glory of God. This is no secret!!!

Romans 3:21-26
God's Righteousness Through Faith

21 But now the righteousness of God apart from the law is revealed, being witnessed by the Law and the Prophets,

22 even the righteousness of God, through faith in Jesus Christ, to all and on all who believe. For there is no difference;

23 for all have sinned and fall short of the glory of God,

24 being justified freely by His grace through the redemption that is in Christ Jesus,

25 whom God set forth as a propitiation by His blood, through faith, to demonstrate His righteousness, because in His forbearance God had passed over the sins that were previously committed,

26 to demonstrate at the present time His righteousness, that He might be just and the justifier of the one who has faith in Jesus.

  Our God is a God of mercy. In the Bible scriptures it records this attribute over and over again and I for one believe it. God has been merciful to me. But the Body of Christ must buckle up, put on the Full Armor of God daily and seek God while He yet may be found. The Body of Christ is changing and will never look the same after this year of 2020 and we must be part of The Remnant that holds fast and endures until the end. There will be great rewards.

  God's mercies endureth forever...

Psalm 136:1
*O give thanks unto the L*ORD*; for he is good: for his mercy endureth for ever.*

How can we go wrong with God's mercies because they endure? They are renewed each and every morning and finally He has given us JESUS as the reprieve, hasn't He? Isn't Jesus the propitiation for our sins? Isn't that so exciting? I am excited to get a reprieve on that day so long ago in 1998 when I accepted Jesus into my heart. But the world continued on even though I started to get cleaned up going from glory to glory with the Lord. I can never take it for granted or forget the impact that moment had on my life as I turned from sin and started on the Potter's Wheel going round and round as God patiently worked with me; still working with me today and I give Him the glory because it is all His and never mine. This book will not be a book or an exercise in futility but a Word of the Lord as I have received it, so shall I give it to you. This word is on me and I must be aware that it is for you too as we walk into 2021 and be prepared that God has spoken here in these words because I have nothing to give but to give from the Spirit of the Living God who instructs me day to day to write. He assigns angels to work with me (Psalm 91:11) and inspires every aspect of this book. It is His after all! Jeremiah spoke it in scripture:

Jeremiah 1:12
Then said the LORD unto me, Thou hast well seen: for I will hasten my word to perform it.

Amen.

Psalm 34:4
I sought the LORD, and he heard me,
and delivered me from all my fears.

AUTHOR'S CORNER

Susan J Perry lives and writes in Edgewater, Florida. She is married to John R Perry and they have 4 children in their blended marriage and 5 grandchildren who live all over the United States of America. They visit as much as they can.

She loves and serves her Lord Jesus Christ knowing only by His Spirit does she write and create page by page. Pure inspiration is so beautiful as the mornings run into nights and nights into mornings as she taps the keyboard on one finger quickly and as accurately as possible. She and her husband now publish books in *Simply This Publishing* and are having a great time doing so. Life is good for both of them. They give God all the praise, the honor and the glory for His loving ways. God is so good!

They have just started on children's books which are a new avenue for them and they hope it will work. They pray and ask God to direct their paths, and the funny thing is He does. God is in the blessing business and today is no different, God never changes, thankfully so.

They attend Edgewater Church of God in Edgewater, Florida with Bishop William T White and they love it there hearing the truth of God's Word. They are active in the church and are very thankful that they now serve locally, helping out as they are able.

Susan and her husband are ordained by Dr Frank and Karen Sumrall of Sumrall Global Ministries of Bristol, Virginia. Their life's call is in the Ministry of Helps to go into churches and help the Pastors wherever help is needed. They have an Aaron and Hur ministry of holding up the arms of the Pastors as they have need.

Exodus 17:12
But Moses' hands became heavy; so they took a stone and put it under him, and he sat on it. And Aaron and Hur supported his hands, one on one side, and the other on the other side; and his hands were steady until the going down of the sun.

Susan speaks at women's groups in churches when invited. They often find themselves in Clearwater or Dunedin, Florida on the west coast while they live on the east coast 3 hours away by car but loving every minute of it. They take their books and often have a product table to set up wherever they go. She and her husband go where the Lord sends them and they are glad to do it. God always provides.

Psalm 100:2
Serve the LORD with gladness; come before his presence with joy.

PERRY'S BOOK SHELF

The Samaritan Woman Testifies
Kindle only: $9.95

Simply This: The World's Greatest Message
Paperback: $5.95 Kindle: $3.99

Preach It Sister Girl!
Paperback: $9.95 Kindle: $5.99

ASK for WISDOM: The Safe Harbor of God
Paperback: $9.95 Kindle: $5.99

A Stone's Throw Away: A Woman Testifies
Paperback: $12.95 Kindle: $6.99

The Persistent Widow Testifies
Paperback: $12.95 Kindle: $6.99

The Woman Presenting the Alabaster Box Testifies
Paperback: $12.95 Kindle: $6.99

Great Holes in Your Pockets: Recovering All!
Paperback: $9.95 Kindle $5.99

Hidden in the Cleft of the Rock: A Woman Testifies
Paperback: $12.95 Kindle: $6.99

Daughters of Inheritance Testify
Paperback: $12.95 Kindle: $6.99

This Project is Called: HONOR
Paperback: $9.95 Kindle: $5.99

Our Experiences With ANGELS
Paperback $9.95 Kindle $5.99

The Double-Dip Blessings
Paperback $9.95 Kindle $5.99

It's Never Too Late To Pray
Paperback $5.95 Kindle $2.99

I AM A DUCK!
Paperback $9.95 Kindle $5.95

The Woman Touching the Hem of His Garment Testifies
Paperback $12.95 Kindle $6.99

This is the Anemic Church
Paperback $9.95 Kindle $5.99

There is a Witness!
Paperback $9.95 Kindle $5.99

Heal Them ALL! The Children's Portion
Paperback $7.95 Kindle $3.99

Ye Shall Serve God On This Mountain!
Paperback $12.95 Kindle $6.99

Thanksgiving is Best!
Paperback $7.95 Kindle $3.99

The ABC'S of Perry
Paperback $12.95

LOVE is Surely The Way
Paperback $7.95 Kindle $3.99

Lessons In Deliverance
Paperback $12.95 Kindle $6.99

ALL BOOKS AVAILABLE ON AMAZON.COM

1 Corinthians 14:3
But he who prophesies speaks edification and exhortation and comfort to men

All available on www.Amazon.com
Kindle Direct Publishing
Simply This Publishing
John & Susan Perry
Edgewater, Florida

Contact info:

Susan J Perry, Email: susiebqt987p@yahoo.com
& Facebook

John R Perry, Email: jperry8@bellsouth.net

Books can also be ordered through bookstores and big box stores if that is your preference. There is always a way.

In Florida our books are available in:

From My Library 2 URS

3510 S Nova Road, Suite # 107

Port Orange, Florida 32129

REFERENCES

Wikipedia online research

Bible Gateway online Bible scripture research

The King James Study Bible for Women

Webster and Oxford Dictionary online definitions

Black & White online free clipart

Amazon online website

No copyright infringement intended

Ephesians 6:10
__Finally, my brethren, be strong in the Lord, and in the power of his might.__

Made in United States
Orlando, FL
23 December 2023